Hiking Around Los Angeles With Joaquin Murrieta

25 Hikes

Volume One

Also by G. Kent

Running with Razors and Soul:
A Handbook for Competitive Runners

Hiking in North Florida with William Bartram:
25 Hikes - Volume One

Hiking in North Florida with William Bartram:
25 Hikes - Volume Two

The Bandit Monologues

Hiking Around Los Angeles With Joaquin Murrieta

25 Hikes

Volume One

G. Kent

© Copyright 2018 by Gary R. Kent

All rights reserved. No part of this book may be used or reproduced by any means, graphic, electronic or mechanical, including photocopying, recording, taping or by any informational storage retrieval system, without the written permission of the publisher, except in the case of brief quotations embodied in critical articles or reviews.

ISBN – 13: 9781984304612
ISBN – 10: 1984304615

Bandit Press
2327 NE 8th Place
Ocala, Florida 34470
kentib@earthlink.net

This book may be ordered from the publisher, through booksellers at Barnes and Noble, or online at Createspace.com or Amazon.com.

CONTENTS

Dedication	viii
"Follow the River" by Michael Riedell	xi
Foreword by Greystone Holt	xii
Introduction	1
Prologue – Hiking with Adults	4
Quotes	6
Image on the Cover	9
Seasons	11
Water	13
What to Carry	15
Wildlife	17
Lost	19
Crime – Firearms	21
Leave it Alone	23
Hike # 1 – The Devil's Chair	24
Hike # 2 – Saddleback Butte	30

Hike # 3 – Vasquez Rocks	35
Hike # 4 – Antelope Valley: California Poppy Preserve	39
Hike # 5 – Placerita Canyon	43
Hike # 6 – Strawberry Peak	47
Hike # 7 – Mt. Baden-Powell	52
Hike # 8 – Mt. Hillyer	55
Hike # 9 – Devil's Canyon	59
Hike # 10 – Cooper Creek Falls	63
Hike # 11 – Halfmoon Campground	67
Hike # 12 – Dome Springs	70
Hike # 13 – Mt. Pinos	73
Hike # 14 – Sawmill Mountain	77
Hike # 15 – Jupiter Peak	81
Hike # 16 – Rice Canyon	85
Hike # 17 – Mission Peak	89
Hike # 18 – La Tuna Canyon	93
Hike # 19 – Chumash Trail	97

Hike # 20 – Simi Peak	100
Hike # 21 – Sandstone Peak	103
Hike # 22 – Lower Solstice Canyon and Sostomo Trail	107
Hike # 23 – Nicholas Flat	111
Hike # 24 – Sycamore and Serrano Canyons	115
Hike # 25 – Mt. Baldy	119
Epilogue – We Have to Care	123
Happy Trails	124
"Los Angeles" by James Abraham Martling	125
Recommended Reading	126

Dedication

"So many tales have grown up around (Joaquin) Murrieta that it is impossible to disentangle the fabulous from the factual."
- Susan Lee Johnson

Thus it is with the city of Los Angeles. Joaquin Murrieta is an ideal symbol of the smoke and mirrors that have created a mysterious and glittering aura surrounding the L.A. metropolis. A Hollywood town with its stories in print or on film—and anyone is permitted to decide what is truth or the fantastic.

Who was Joaquin Murrieta? He may have actually been a composite of at least three individuals, but I doubt it. Born in Hermosillo, Mexico, he moved his family to California during the Gold Rush and immediately encountered racism and violence. Legends assert he was driven off a rich claim, his wife raped, half-brother lynched and himself brutally horse-whipped. These actions, if true, may have forced him into a life of banditry, which many sociologists contend is an act of social rebellion by the oppressed toward their oppressors in Latin America. Many bandits were local heroes. Pushed roughly into a corner by powerful social and economic forces, Murrieta's only option was to strike back as an outlaw. Other researchers claim Murrieta was actually a Mexican patriot who fought to bring California back under Mexican control. To local California Hispanics, Murrieta symbolized Mexican resistance to Anglo culture and economic dominance. Murrieta reportedly was not an Anglo hater; indeed he had many Anglo friends. But he did desire California to be under Mexican sovereignty.

The California State Legislature in Sacramento sought to curb Murrieta's activities and hired twenty California Rangers, all veterans of the Mexican-American War, led by Captain Harry S. Love, a former Texas Ranger, to hunt down and exterminate Murrieta and his gang. The rangers attacked an armed band of Mexicans in the coastal range near Coalinga, north of Mt. Pinos, and killed several bandits, including Murrieta and his partner Three-Fingered Jack. As proof for Sacramento officials, the head of Murrieta and hand of Three-Fingered Jack were severed and brought back to the capital. Legend has it the rangers actually killed an innocent Mexican horseman and bribed seventeen locals, including a Catholic priest, to swear to the identity of the head. Stories quickly spread of sightings of Murrieta as an older man hiding out in the Tehachapi Mountains near Fort Tejon. Also, it is still rumored that Murrieta's head floats through the air and haunts the mountains of the southern Los Padres National Forest.

Nevertheless, Murrieta was hailed as the Robin Hood of El Dorado and, along with Tiburcio Vasquez and Manual Garcia (Three-Fingered Jack), became the basis for the popular Zorro myth.

This book is dedicated to the legend, spirit, phantasm and memory of Joaquin Murrieta (1829-1853), whose mythic stature and fantastical reputation could rightfully be symbolic of the City of Angels.

Follow the River

Follow from its ocean mouth
the river inland
up through mountains,
through gorges and twists,
through stony shallows, pools, forks,
upward,
then up further
to where rush becomes gurgle
and water sometimes flows below
forest loam,
where streamlets start
as morning mist beading,
trickling from leaves of madrone:

Here I have my home. Here I am
a student of beginnings and trajectory,
of saplings and dreams.

- Michael Riedell

From *The Way of Water,* Slow Mountain Press, 2014.

Foreword

"Thousands of tired, nerve-shaken, over-civilized people are beginning to find out that going to a mountain is going home."
- John Muir

The amazing thing about this hiking book is that every trail is within 30 minutes to two hours of any street in Los Angeles. They're all easy day hikes. Beaches, mountains and desert—that's what's so awesome and magical about the area surrounding L.A. Yes, I said magical. If the L.A. experience is injected into your bloodstream, you will delight in the magical nature of the city. Native-born Angelinos know exactly what I'm talking about.

I've never met a more enthusiastic and dedicated hiker than G. Kent. But what makes him unique is what people say about him. Friends refer to him as a "wilderness mystic." I'm not exactly sure what that means. He's not pretentious or some enigmatic figure. He's fun loving and adventuresome. But there's a higher quality about him—something indefinable and mystifying. I just think he hears and sees things in the wilderness that most people don't notice. Come along with G. Kent on these hikes and you will be introduced to an entirely new and mysterious world. It's not just hiking or enjoying an adult beverage, it's touching and appreciating the natural world, and reveling in life.

    Los Angeles is the city and G. Kent takes you to its soul.

Greystone Holt
Topanga Canyon

P.S. – I'm a tad disappointed he didn't include a trail in Topanga Canyon State Park.

P.P.S. – Perhaps not. Let it be our little secret.

Introduction

"There's something almost haunted about Los Angeles, a vibrant mythology I find rather inspiring."
  - Heidi Slimane

Los Angeles is my hometown and its mystique courses through my veins. Of course I dislike smog, traffic and lunatic hordes. I ran track and cross country in high school and sucked down the filthy air on a daily basis as if it were a carton of Camels. But the streets of L.A. are lined with palms, eucalyptus and fir trees, and the air is tinged with sage, coastal cedar and Pacific spray. The streets are normally drenched in golden sunshine while the sky appears to drip with luminous clouds and blue honey. It's like living in a Salvador Dali painting.

David Thompson imagined Los Angeles as "Marilyn Monroe, fifty miles long, lying on her side, and half-buried on a ridge of crumbling rock." I like that. Is L.A. a paradise? Of course not. However, I have a philosophy about L.A. haters—if you're from L.A. you have a right to criticize, but if you're from out-of-town you need to shut your mouth or go back to New Jersey. Don't be part of the problem. The best way to help the place where we live is to be happy we live there.

When Los Angeles became part of the United States its population was about 3000. Can you imagine? L.A. was always a backwater during the Spanish-Mexican eras. Its Mission de San Fernando, though harmonious and serene, is perhaps the most unimpressive of the twenty-one missions built by Father Junipero Sierra. However, the twentieth century witnessed L.A. becoming home base to an eclectic population including Raymond Chandler and Charles Bukowski, Kathryn Hepburn and Humphrey Bogart, Mickey Cohen and Bugsy Siegel, Sandy Koufax, Magic Johnson and the rock bands The Byrds, The Doors and Crosby, Stills, Nash and Young. The city can shock, dazzle, delight and horrify. It's mystifying and remarkable. Jack Kerouac wrote, "I love the way everybody says 'L.A.' on the Coast; it's their one and only golden town when all is said and done." It's a golden town with glittering boulevards, sparkling beaches, rolling hills and snow-capped mountains. Raymond Chandler said the City of Angels evokes "murderous moods fed by the Santa Ana winds, all Hollywood mystery and film noir."

That's what L.A. is—film noir.

Here are my twenty-five favorite hikes around Los Angeles. I believe Joaquin Murrieta would approve. Three million people live in L.A., ten million in L.A. County and nineteen million in the megalopolis. Hopefully these trails, in close proximity to such mobs of humanity, will make you feel like you're in remote and secluded parcels of paradise where "you can forget all your troubles, forget all your cares…"

Lace up your hiking boots and join Joaquin Murrieta and me for some rollicking and spontaneous fun on the trails.

Prologue – Hiking With Adults

> *"L.A. is a flash and a mountain lion, Venice Beach and Santa Monica Pier, a Hollywood sign, surf, sunshine and the Dodgers."*
> — L. G. Larson

> *"Wine is constant proof that God loves us and loves to see us happy."*
> — Ben Franklin

This hiking book is for adults, whether it be the guys, ladies, couples or soloists. Living the daily grind can be quite stressful. Adult life is both difficult and challenging, and stress is a common result that can cause an array of maladies including anxiety, depression, headaches, stomachaches or simple frustration. One super way to deal with these assorted ills is to go outdoors and enjoy the beauty and wonder of the natural world.

Unfortunately, the presence of children on a trail can hinder adult thought, adult conversation and adult activities. Some of those activities may include an adult beverage or a blanket for adult shenanigans.

You are not being a selfish or irresponsible parent for desiring a short down time away from the kiddies. In fact, if adults are stressed out and unhappy with their lives, that can adversely affect their ability to raise the children.

If you must have a child along on your hike, bring Bowser. He's a kid in a dog suit, and I guarantee he'll enjoy and appreciate the trail much more than the three-year old.

Adults require and deserve the right to decompress from their daily stressful lives. What better place to relax than on a beautiful hiking trail around Los Angeles?

Quotes

"Hating L.A. is a form of snobbery. It's a 'I'm from the civilized East Coast and what is this place?' kind of snootiness."
— Ice Cold Lemonade

I wanted to put in complementary quotes praising Los Angeles at the beginning of each section of the book but, low and behold, I had horrendous difficulty finding any. It appears no one likes L.A. One site advertised "32 great quotes about Los Angeles" and every one was a derogatory zinger.

I was baffled.

People come to L.A. and then miss their hometown in Indiana. You've got to be kidding! They bemoan that everyone in L.A. is from somewhere else. Not true! Generations of native-born Angelinos populate the L.A. basin, including me. Newcomers complain about the phony, plastic and hypocritical culture, then lap it up with a spoon and toss their souls into the mix. They enjoy the beaches, mountains, lifestyles, nightlife, opportunities and weather – then whine about the freeways. Huh? That's like whining about the wind. Smog? Good grief! Most of it comes from your cars. Ride a bike!

Here are some examples along with my comments:

"Traffic is God-awful." Really? Have you ever driven in Atlanta or D.C.?

"L.A. is the loneliest and most brutal of American cities." I'm certain everyone in Newark wants to be my friend.

"Downtown L.A. is squalid." No, it's not. That proves you never go there because it has been lovingly restored. Try touring Gary, Indiana.

"A regular hell is L.A." No, that's El Paso.

"The entrance to the underworld is L.A." So what? That sounds kinda cool.

"I don't like L.A. The people are awful…and everyone wants to be famous. I'm from NYC. I will kill to get what I want." Thank you for clarifying.

Some of the nastiest quotes about Los Angeles come from a clown named Bret Easton Ellis. Who the hell is he? Let's Google him because some of his quotes make me want to punch him in the nose. Let's see: Generation X writer and author of *American Psycho*. His characters are aware of their depravity, but choose to enjoy it. Sounds like a perfectly sane person. But hold on—born in Los Angeles and grew up in Sherman Oaks. Holy cow! He's a Valley dude, like me. I sincerely apologize, brother. Now I want to read your books. Remember: if you're from L.A., you can say what you want—it's your birthright. If you move to L.A., you need to be polite or get the hell out!

Go Dodgers, Bret!

Image on the Cover

"The setting sun burned the sky pink and orange in the same brilliant hues as surfers bathing suits. Sunsets did that in L.A., made you forget it was the smog that made those colors so brilliant, that behind every pretty picture there could be an ugly story."
- Michael Connelly

Please take another peek at the image of Los Angeles on our front cover. Wow! Denver and Seattle do not have finer skyline vistas.

True, at times the sky is hazy, and at other times it's extremely hazy. Yet there are days when Los Angeles will emerge in its full glory and dazzle like in the photo.

The tallest building in L.A. is the U.S. Bank Tower at 1018 feet and 73 floors, soon to be outdone by the Wilshire Grand Center at 1027 feet. I believe there are still height limits due to earthquakes. Notice the iconic L.A. city hall, which is dwarfed, on the right. For forty years (1928-1968) city hall was the tallest building (32 stories) in Los Angeles and featured in countless movies and TV shows, including *Dragnet*.

To the east, far above the skyline, lie the San Gabriel Mountains with Mt. Lukens and San Gabriel Peak dominating the view. On the other side of the San

Gabriels is the vast upper Mojave Desert. Do an about face and you'll be staring at Palos Verde Point, Santa Catalina Island and the Pacific Ocean.

Are you familiar with the Los Angeles trifecta? I've experienced it once in my life. In the month of January, I got up at 5:00 a.m. and by 7:00 a.m. I had paddled out in full wetsuit next to the Santa Monica pier and surfed for two hours. Back home at 10:00 a.m. for a shower and early lunch, and then back on the road for skiing on Mt. Waterman by 1:30 p.m. Finally, I cruised down the Little Tujunga Highway and enjoyed a glass of wine for sunset at Saddleback Butte State Park in the Mojave Desert. Home by 8:30 p.m.

Try it. You'll have an incredible day.

Seasons

"I read in Life Magazine articles about free love and free dope... at age 20 I drove to L.A."
- Glenn Frey

Seasons are something Los Angeles hikers do not have to be concerned about. L.A. has no bad hiking season. It's even fun to be out in the rain. Hike just about anywhere at any time. My only warning is to stay out of the Mojave Desert during summer, and of course be aware of wildfire, flash flood and mudslide warnings.

If it's too hot in the Basin, head up to the San Gabriels or Tehachapis. If it's too icy cold in the mountains, head down to the beaches or Santa Monicas. If the rain has set in during winter, the sunny Mojave Desert is calling. Although there can be thunderstorms in the mountains during summer, rainy season in L.A. is mostly winter and spring. I *always* bring lightweight rain gear or a windbreaker with hood on hikes regardless of the weather report. Besides being great for the rain, either article can add warmth or be nice to spread out on the ground to sit.

I get so weary when I hear people boast about how much nicer San Francisco is than L.A. It's not. I like San Francisco; it's a cultured, exciting and fascinating town. It has hills and is surrounded by water, just like L.A. Only L.A.'s hills and mountains get snow-capped and are more scenic. Also, Angelinos can swim and surf comfortably at our beaches. Here's the skinny: San Francisco's weather is dreadful. It has two seasons—cold and foggy. While visiting San Francisco in summer, my wife and I were forced to stop at The Gap to buy fleece sweatshirts because we weren't prepared for temps in the mid-50s. I don't want to make this a war between the two cities. I like 'em both. Why can't people from S.F. like L.A.?

What is there to say about New York? To compare seasons or appearance between New York and Los Angeles is not only incomprehensible, it's idiotic. I'm sorry, Woody Allen, but NYC is gross.

Water

"It's a different kind of hot in Los Angeles, the kind that made the Beach Boys all tan and giddy, a heat that doesn't harass you in the shade."
  - Caroline Kepnes

Water. Between 1902-1913 Los Angeles, under the corrupt leadership of William Mulholland (yes, of Mulholland Drive fame) and Fred Eaton, mayor of L.A., a vicious water war was conducted with Owens Valley in northern California that culminated in the construction of the L.A.-Owens Valley Aqueduct to bring Sierra Nevada water to a thirsty and growing Los Angeles. Chicanery and "a strategy of lies" contributed to the victory. The treacherous battle for water was the subject matter for Roman Polanski's brilliant film *Chinatown*, starring Jack Nicholson, Faye Dunaway and John Huston.

My point? Water is king in L.A.

On a hike around Los Angeles, water is the most important item in your daypack. Always bring more than you think you'll need because, as we Angelinos know, you can never have enough. On several occasions, I have supplied water to thirsty hikers on the trail. I've had people offer money for a bottle of water.

Once, in Joshua Tree National Park, I ran out of water and it was not pretty. Lesson learned. If you're concerned about weight, leave the beer at home. Never cut down on water.

I've witnessed hikers heading uphill in ninety-five degree weather without packs or any visible signs of water. Either they weren't serious hikers or not very smart, and they may have soon been in serious trouble. Also, don't think you only need water when it's hot. Temperature has little to do with your body's craving for agua. Always drink more than you think you need. Remember: if you're thirsty, you may already be dehydrated.

Side note: unless you're in absolute survival mode, do not drink untreated surface water. You could become sick beyond description and it's not worth the risk. The water may appear crystal clear and potable—but don't drink it!

What To Carry

"Sometimes I feel like my only friend is the city I live in, the city of angels lonely as I am. Together we cry."

— Red Hot Chili Peppers

Every hiking book has its special list of what to carry on a day hike. Mine is ordinary and certainly not complete. One item I recommend that most books leave out is a lightweight folding chair. Any aluminum contraption will work. This may sound burdensome, but when you're ready to relax with an adult beverage a chair is sweet.

Also:

Hat	Snacks
Sunglasses	Water
Sunscreen	Knife
Bug spray	Extra T-shirt
Raingear	Extra socks
Flashlight	Whistle
Fleece or sweatshirt	Map
Compass	First aid kit
Matches or lighter	Book or magazine

The extra T-shirt is to replace the sweaty one after your hike in. If it's cold, a wet T-shirt can be miserable. Extra socks are in case you stumble through water, mud or snow.

Now for the secret stuff. A small blanket or sheet is great for naps or sex. Yes, I said sex. If the mood and location are right, and weather cooperates, sex in the wild can be exhilarating and delightful. Also, bring your favorite adult beverage. Whether it's beer, wine or spirits, an adult beverage will enhance the experience. You want it cold? Most stores have excellent small and collapsible coolers that will fit snuggly into any daypack. Or try my little trick. Take a one-gallon zip lock baggy and add ice with your favorite beer or wine, or use the ice for cocktails. The bag may leak slightly, but it is well worth the inconvenience.

Wildlife

"Nobody really likes L.A., they put up with it. But it's good to be in the belly of the beast."
- Robo Burgi

The wildlife in the Los Angeles area is exquisite, but please remember that the key word here is "wild." Wild animals are untamed and unpredictable. You're not on a ride at Disneyland or Universal. You will be safe by leaving them alone. Bear or mountain lion will not start a fight, but most know how to finish one. Be smart and give all wild animals their space. Observe, photograph and enjoy, but stay back. If confronted, always stand your ground and make yourself appear larger. Make plenty of noise.

A few of the L.A. stars:

Coyote – 20 to 50 pounds. They travel solo or in packs, and will eat practically anything. Their haunting yips and howls liven up the backcountry. They will usually run if you approach or make noise—that's why they're so good at adaption and survival.

Mountain lion – 80 to 160 pounds. Solitary and elusive creatures that avoid human contact at nearly all costs. You will be fortunate to spot one with its black-tipped tail and ears. Never run from a mountain lion, it will trigger their instinct to chase. Stand tall, wave your arms and make noise. Remember: mountain lions are federally protected.

Black or brown bear – 200 to 600 pounds. Though the grizzly bear graces our state flag, the species has been extinct in California since August 1922. But we have plenty of black and brown bears. Bears are extremely intelligent, solitary and wary of people. Good bears always run from humans. However, all bears will take advantage of a free meal. Never feed a bear. A fed bear is a dead bear. A problem bear will likely be destroyed. Take extra precaution around cubs.

Bobcat, mule deer, red fox, raccoons and skunk.

Birds too numerous to list. My favorites are all species of hawk and owl, golden eagles, California condors and the feisty grouse. The California quail is the state bird.

Snakes – Most people are terrified of snakes, yet most species are benign and helpful for the environment. California has seven species of rattlesnakes, but all are shy and prefer to retreat when encountered. Most snake bites occur when people attempt to kill, capture or pick one up, and most bites are on the hands or lower legs. Simply watch your step and retreat if a snake is sighted. When left alone, snakes pose no danger.

Check out the marine life along the coast, including whale, seal and dolphin.

Let's review: Do not approach a bobcat or try to pick up a snake. No selfies with bear. Photograph and enjoy.

Lost

"I've never been lost, but I was mighty turned around for three days once."
— Daniel Boone

"My grandmother started walking five miles a day when she was 90. She's 93 today, and we don't know where the hell she is."
— Ellen DeGeneres

You're hiking with a group, and then you stop for a pee break. "Go on," you say, "I'll catch up." After all, everyone requires a little privacy. It takes three minutes and you're on your way, but soon you reach a fork in the trail with no sign. You go left and hike fast for twenty minutes, but you don't catch up. You go right at another fork and hike for ten minutes. Nothing.

What to do?

Or you're hiking alone to a special point of interest. It's only three miles. You think you've followed the right trail, but you've hiked for over an hour and know you should have reached your destination. You come to a junction and go right for another twenty minutes. Nothing. You believe you're close to your spot, but suddenly feel confused and uncomfortable.

What to do?

First off, don't hike any farther. Try to retrace your steps. If you think you are lost, DO NOT LEAVE THE TRAIL! Here are my nine steps to follow:

1. Breathe and relax. Look around. Don't worry.
2. Take an inventory of your pack, just in case. Hopefully you'll find water, food, matches, knife, raingear and a warm top. If you have that stuff, you'll be okay.
3. Make noise. Clap your hands or blow the whistle. Yelling usually won't be heard and will give you a sore throat.
4. Look for landmarks and other people.
5. Never try a shortcut or leave the trail.
6. Don't run or panic. Don't quit mentally.
7. If you can start a small fire, do so in a contained area. Smoke might be seen.
8. Forget the movies. Roving packs of animals or backwoods mutants will not murder you. Weather will be your biggest threat.
9. If you become exhausted, stop hiking. If you keep trying to hike, you'll become even more fatigued, disoriented and grumpy.

Chin up. Put on your game face. People are probably already looking for you. You will get out of this with a great story.

Crime and Firearms

"Go back to Jersey, sonny. This is the City of Angels and you haven't got any wings."
- Charles Dudley Smith,
L.A Confidential

Warning signs at trailheads are common. An example:
"Did you leave: cellphone, Ipod, CDs, purse or wallet in car? It won't be there when you get back."

You can also get a broken window or flat tire. Your poor car is vulnerable sitting by itself at a remote trailhead. For the most part, thieves and pinheaded vandals know where you are and know they suffer little risk conducting their nefarious deeds.

Take valuables with you or put 'em in the trunk—or leave 'em at home.

The Angeles National Forest has been labeled the most dangerous and crime-ridden national forest in the nation. What can you expect when a recreational forest is adjacent to nineteen million people? Consider the possibilities if a national forest were 15-30 minutes from Detroit or Chicago.

I'd rather not shock or horrify anyone with details or statistics, but the majority of crimes in the Angeles are minor (vandalism, drunk and disorderly, car break-ins and fisticuffs), and the vast majority of crimes occur in campgrounds, picnic grounds or other day-use areas. With regard to crime, a forest trail is probably one of the safest places in the world. Serial killers usually don't take time off to hike a nature trail. Trust me: trail hiking around Los Angeles is a safe venture.

Should you bring a firearm along for protection? I wouldn't deter you if it makes you feel more secure, but I certainly wouldn't bring a firearm out of fear of the wildlife. Animals run away from humans. If you shot a bear, you'd probably only piss him off—then you could be in real trouble. I personally don't believe carrying a firearm is worth the risk. Statistics clearly indicate that I'm far more likely to shoot a friend or myself rather than an evildoer. If you disagree, I respect that—but why be part of the problem? Stay alert and practical around strangers. There's no need for paranoia on the trail.

Leave It Alone

"L.A. is always a good idea."
- Fis Robin

Please do not deface or take any natural feature or historical artifact from any of our parks or preserves.

Please do not litter. It's like a spit in the face to America.

Kill nothing but time.

Leave only footprints, take only photos and memories.

Hike # 1

The Devil's Chair

"Time to put the dust back on the boots, folks."
- Bunk Henry

Directions – From the San Fernando Valley drive north on the 405. Take Highway 14 (Antelope Valley Freeway) to Palmdale. Exit on Pearblossom Highway/California 138 and drive east to Little Rock. Turn right (south) on N6 and follow signs.

Devil's Punchbowl County Park is a 1310-acre geological wonder in the upper Mojave one hour from the San Fernando Valley. It's at 4740 feet elevation and the bowl is 300 feet deep. Try to visit after a light dusting of snow. The Punchbowl's tilted and pillowed rocks were formed by San Gabriel Mountains water runoff, and the bowl sits in the shadows of its towering peaks. The Devil's Punchbowl is as stunning as any natural feature in our National Parks system.

The finest view within the Punchbowl's spectacular heap of rocks is at a precarious point of jutting stone known as the Devil's Chair. The hike to the chair is a six-mile round trip with a steady but manageable ascent along with viewpoints galore.

You'll share the terrain with mountain lion, bear, coyote, bobcat and gray fox. Golden eagle, ravens and hawk soar overhead. The trail will lead from the high desert of juniper, chaparral and pinyon pine to yellow pine, coulter/digger pine and bigcone Douglas fir. Boy, somebody really messed up those names. Bigcone Douglas fir have medium-sized cones while coulter/digger pine cones resemble bowling balls with spikes. You will be knocked into the next week if one of those cannonballs conks you on the noggin—and it's the heaviest cone in the world.

Side trip # 1 – One mile up the trail is a turnoff on the right for the Burkhart Trail, which winds along a steep ridge among the pines before turning south and climbing Pleasant View Ridge all the way up to the Angeles Crest Highway. I suggest a short venture of 0.5 miles along the ridge. It's mostly flat and the views of the upper Mojave and Tehachapi Mountains to the north or the San Gabriels to the south will give you inner peace. Plus, you'll be alone. I've never met another hiker on this trail. Return to the main trail and continue toward the Devil's Chair. On a recent outing to the Burkhart Trail, a ranger in the empty parking lot stared at me in disbelief and said, "Son, do you know it's seventeen degrees?" I hiked 0.5 miles on the Burkhart and then decided to climb nearly straight up to a patch of snow under several large Douglas firs. It was a more difficult climb than it looked. I plopped down on the snow and nearly fell asleep. If I did not come down, I have no doubt my body would still be up there today.

Side trip # 2 – At 1.5 miles the trail crosses Punchbowl Creek, which is an excellent resting spot coming or going. Try bushwhacking up the creek for a little water fun. I've discovered numerous isolated spots for reading, writing or meditation.

After another 1.5 miles of winding ascent, where you'll pass several other boulders worthy to bag, you'll reach a short spur trail on the left (north) that leads to the Devil's Chair. Visit, but don't stay. Someone came up with the idiotic idea to construct a hideous five-foot chain-link fence around the entire perimeter of the point to keep pinheaded adventurers from falling into the abyss. Holy cow, Batman, it feels like being tossed into the hoosegow. It's uncomfortable and creepy to stand at the vista point, especially if you're forced to share the small area with other hikers. It's also, in my opinion, unnecessary. Signs warn that people have fallen to their deaths. What else is needed? I'm for safety and protecting the stupid, but there are plenty of other spots where numbskulls can hand their beers to a friend and clamber dangerously close to oblivion. Take the fence down and leave the Devil's Chair in its natural state, I say. Nevertheless, go back to the main trail and choose one of the many other lonely boulders with equally breathtaking views of the Punchbowl without the unsightly fence and eat your lunch.

Incidentally, it's called the Punchbowl because the large white granite boulders strewn about resemble large ice cubes.

Wherever you choose to relax, you'll enjoy stunning views of desert, vast mountain ranges and brilliant sky. Beware of the devil—he could be skulking about ready to lounge on his chair or offer you a deal for your soul. It makes me chuckle how desert beauty is often associated with devilish names. Devil's Playground, Hell's Furnace, Satan's Funhouse. Where do angels go to hike?

On a recent visit to the Devil's Chair, I had the prison cell to myself because it was late in the afternoon. The thud of hiking boots announced the arrival of company. When I glanced up the trail, I saw an odd-looking young fellow with spiked hair and thick glasses. He lugged an impressive-looking leather briefcase. I recognized him immediately: he was James E. Lindsay—Bigfoot Researcher.

We stared at one another in disbelief.

"You!" he cried. "What are *you* doing in California?"

"Hello, James," I said. "I grew up in Los Angeles. Care for a cup of wine?"

I had met James E. Lindsay earlier in the year near Ocklawaha Prairie in Florida. He had been investigating what was considered to be a credible sighting of two Bigfoot by a couple of Belleview schoolteachers.

I said, "You're not still mad because I scoffed at your investigation on the prairie, are you?"

"Nope," he said. "My interview with the couple went well and will be published in *Outside* magazine." He took a sip of wine.

"Congratulations," I said, grinning. "Are you conducting an investigation at the Punchbowl?"

He looked up. "You've heard the stories?"

I nodded.

"On April 22, 1973 three men spotted a ten-foot tall Bigfoot up Big Lock Creek near South Fork Campground about four miles from this spot. It had a six-foot stride and twenty-one- inch tracks—that's a real big boy. The one in the 1966 Patterson film was only seven feet tall with a sixteen-inch footprint. The men reported the sighting to the sheriff department in Lancaster, and soon scores of hunters were scouring the area with high-powered rifles. From that day, dozens of sightings have occurred in the area. In fact, my organization believes it's a special species of Bigfoot with three toes instead of five."

"What are you investigating today?"

"Three weeks ago, two college girls saw an ape-like figure among the scree from this very spot. They called to it and it seemed to acknowledge their presence. The girls even left beef jerky and crackers as an offering."

That did it! When James mentioned beef jerky, I immediately pictured those idiotic commercials with a Bigfoot tossing juvenile pranksters into the air. I fought it mightily, but couldn't stop myself from bursting with laughter.

"Dude," I chortled, "that story is so lame."

James frowned. "You'll never be a believer."

"I guess not," I said. "Sorry, dude."

He finished his wine and shut his briefcase. "I'm outta here."

It was dark and I was alone in a remote area where a Bigfoot had recently been sighted. A coyote started to yip.

Bigfoot, I thought. Yeah, right.

I corked my wine bottle. "Hey, James," I shouted. "Wait up."

Hike # 2

Saddleback Butte

"The desert reveals its true character only to those who come with courage, tolerance and understanding. For those, the desert holds rare gifts."
— Randall Henderson

Directions – From the San Fernando Valley drive north on the 405. Take Highway 14 (Antelope Valley Freeway) to Lancaster and head north off 20th Street exit. Turn right (east) on Avenue J and drive 18 miles to the park. Turn right at sign to campground and park in day use-area.

With all the magnificent desert parks in Southern California (Joshua Tree, Death Valley, Mojave National Preserve and Anza-Borrego), this little gem of a state park is often overlooked, and it's only an hour and a half drive from the San Fernando Valley. The park is a mystical magic tour loaded with tons of Joshua Trees and dominated by the twin peaks of Saddleback Butte. You'll either be alone or share the park with only a handful of people.

The name Saddleback Butte may cause you to think the park was named after a medical condition, like tennis elbow, since many suffer from a sore butt after a full day in the saddle. However, this butte is pronounced "beaut," just like Butte, Montana. Sorry kids—there is no Butt, Montana.

This stark and enchanting desert state park was established in 1960 and has 2955 acres of lush Joshua tree habitat, plus its startling butte, which can be seen fifteen miles down the road. Coyotes, kit fox, desert tortoise, jack and cottontail rabbit, badger, skunk and even deer roam the beige terrain, while golden eagle, hawk, raven and owl patrol the skies. Be aware that sidewinder and green Mojave (deadliest of all rattlers) rattlesnakes are present, but rarely seen, even in summer. At one time the grounds were covered with antelope (hence the name Antelope Valley), but unregulated hunting and the railroad (antelope inexplicably refused to cross the tracks) contributed to their demise.

Also, a different kind of bird soars in the sky above Saddleback Butte. In December 2006, I witnessed two stealth bombers coming in at a low altitude on their way to Palmdale Airport. Later, the jets performed a flyover at the Rose Bowl.

Obviously, the best times of the year to visit Saddleback Butte are fall, winter and spring. Summer months can be boiling. I prefer winter. You will experience sunny skies with temps in the 40s. Sunsets on top of the butte can be mind-altering. Bring your flashlight and hike back to your car at dusk.

The trail to the twin peaks is only four miles round trip, with an elevation gain of 1000 feet. Both peaks are slightly over 3600 feet with the larger one on the left (NE) coming in at 3651 feet. I also recommend the short side trail to Little Butte on the return trip. It's about 0.25 miles off the main trail and has excellent views of the Big Butte and surrounding Joshua trees, many specimens are quite large and impressive.

The hike begins at the day-use parking lot next to the small campground. Pay the fee and lock your car. The trail heads directly east toward the center of the butte's saddleback. The first mile is somewhat flat but very sandy. Push on and watch for the side trail to Little Butte on the left. After about a mile, the climb begins. The rocky granite trail is well marked with yellow posts and its ascent can be heart pounding. Stop often, both to catch your breath and enjoy the views. Remember: hiking is supposed to be pleasurable. When you reach the saddleback, try to locate the California aqueduct flowing west to south and bringing much needed water to a thirsty Los Angeles basin. Also, admire the stately Joshuas from the high altitude. The trees resemble an army of alien invaders.

Every trail guide recommends turning left at the saddleback and following the stone-marked trail to the top of the eastern peak. I prefer the southwestern peak to the right. The trail isn't marked, but it's obvious. If you have time, hike both. At the top of either peak, the

360 degrees views of the knife-edged San Gabriel Mountains (including Mt. Baldy) to the south, Mojave Desert to the east, lights of Lancaster and Palmdale to the west and rugged Tehachapis to the north are spectacular. Also, to the north, if the air quality in the San Joaquin Valley cooperates, the distant snow-capped Sierra Nevadas are visible. Remain on top until the first star appears. Star gazing at any location inside the park is awesome.

Sidenote – I met the finest campground host in the nation at Saddleback Butte. (Many hosts tend to be power-hungry tyrants.) I had my German Shepherd along for the hike and then saw a sign warning that dogs are not allowed on the trails in the park. I knocked on the door to the host's camper.

"Morning, sir," I said.
"How are you today, son?"
"Air has a bite."
He smiled. "That's because it's thirty degrees."
"I got a little problem," I admitted. "I didn't know about the dog rule and brought my Shepherd along for the hike. I don't think I can leave him in the car alone for that long."
The host rubbed his chin. "I'll keep him in my RV."
I tilted my head. "Really? That's mighty nice. Thank you."

He looked at the empty parking lot and said, "Oh hell, go ahead and take him with you. He can't hurt nuthin'. Ranger isn't even on duty today."

We shook hands. "You are cool!" I said.

Hike # 3

Vasquez Rocks

"In L.A., everyone is a star."
   - Denzel Washington

Directions – From the San Fernando Valley drive north on the 405. Take Highway 14 (Antelope Valley Freeway) for 12 miles and exit on Agua Dulce Canyon Road. Follow signs to park.

No piece of Los Angeles County is more "wild west" than the spectacular granite outcrops near Agua Dulce named after the 19th century cattle rustler and stagecoach robber Tiburcio Vasquez. The tilted "hogback" ridges in this rugged 932 acre Natural Area Park in the Sierra Pelona Mountains of northern L.A. County have been seen in countless TV oaters and B-western films since the 1930s. The steeply inclined picturesque rocks were formed by rapid erosion, earthquakes and other "slippage" activity along the famous San Andreas Fault.

The area also has a distinct mythical quality. Several Native American sites are on the property. The peaceful Tataviam lived in grass hut villages at Vasquez Rocks when the Spanish first arrived. The last Tataviam died in 1916. For the most part the tribe was assaulted, enslaved and liquidated by soldiers, greedy settlers and overzealous missionaries.

Tiburcio Vasquez (1835-1975) was one of the many notorious bandits during perhaps California's most wild and lawless era, and he often eluded capture by hiding out among these fabulous rocks. Although Vasquez came from a privileged family and easily could have been a rancher, lawyer or even politician, he chose banditry as a form of social and economic protest (much like Joaquin Murrieta) and dreamed of reclaiming California from the invading Yankees.

Reputedly the heroic character Zorro is a composite of Vasquez, Murrieta and Three-Fingered Jack.

Vasquez claimed his crimes were a result of corruption and racial discrimination, and insisted he was a defender of Mexican rights and values. Cattle thievery, highway robbery, burglary and frequent public brawls were his major offenses. He swore he never killed a man. Following a robbery, his trademark shenanigan was to "bind his victims hands behind their backs and leave them face down in the dirt," often unclothed. He spent numerous years in prison, including San Quentin, and was extremely popular among the Mexican-American community who supplied him with food, hideouts and alibis. He was also a notorious ladies man who wrote fancy notes and poetry to his women friends. Many of his stagecoach and other highway robberies took place in the Newhall-Santa Clarita areas all the way up to Acton and

Palmdale along the present route of Highway 14. The rocks that bear his name were a natural hiding spot that could be well guarded and fortified by a relatively small bandit army. Treasure hunters still scour the Vasquez Rocks Natural Area for gold coins and a 500-pound silver ingot that Vasquez purportedly stole from Nevada senator William Morris Stewart and dropped down into a crevice shortly before his death. Sources claim Vasquez seduced and impregnated the niece of a prominent family that had hidden him on a ranch near present-day Melrose Place in Hollywood. The uncle turned Vasquez in and he was sentenced to hang.

Vasquez once said, "A spirit of hatred and revenge took possession of me. I had numerous fights in defense of what I believed to be my rights and those of my countrymen. I believed we were unjustly deprived of the social rights that belonged to us."

When asked just before he was hung if he believed in an afterlife, Vasquez replied, "I hope so … for then soon I shall see all my old sweethearts again."

TV westerns such as *Bonanza, Gunsmoke, Zorro, The Lone Ranger, Have Gun Will Travel* and *The Rifleman* are among the scores of shows that featured the Vasquez Rocks in episodes. More recently two Star Trek films, one in 1994 starring William Shatner and Patrick Stewart and another in 2009 starring Chris Pine and Zoe Saldano, were filmed at the rocks, as was the 2001 *Planet of the Apes* starring Mark Wahlberg, Tim Roth and Helena Bonham Carter.

Coincidentally, Vasquez Rocks is one of the finest star gazing locations in the entire nation with numerous reported UFO sightings.

Oh yeah—the hike! Sorry about that. You can hike, wander, roam or climb in just about any direction you care to explore. The entire Natural Area is extraordinarily alluring and fascinating. The Pacific Crest Trail crosses the park, but noise from Highway 14 is a major annoyance. I'd stick to the rock climbing, which is as good as anything in Joshua Tree National Park. First timers and seasoned pros will find many easy or challenging routes among the slanted rocks. Trails circle the rocks and provide outstanding views of the surrounding area. Enjoy!

Hike # 4

Antelope Valley California Poppy Preserve

"The Angels saw one region where more sunshine lingered than its share, and they came each with a Heaven-made cup to dip into the yellow surplus: Behold - the cups themselves were turned to gold, and there they be, their gold for the golden skies to till."
— Sadie B. Melcalf

Directions – From the San Fernando Valley, drive north on I-5 for 68 miles to CA-138E. Turn east and follow signs to the preserve.

Along the drive up I-5 you'll notice golden poppies and other wildflowers carpeting the Gormon Hills and beyond, the very same hills where in 1991 the artist Christo set up 1,760 yellow umbrellas in a dazzling display of artwork. The umbrellas may be gone, but in spring between the Gormon Hills and Antelope Valley California Poppy Preserve is the largest concentration of California poppies in the world—much prettier than manmade umbrellas.

If you are a Californian (or not), you must at some point in your life visit this park, March to April, to witness these poppies in bloom. Talk about the wow factor! The poppy is the California state flower. The Spanish called the poppy *copa de oro,* or cup of gold. In fact, the poppy IS California. The golden flower symbolizes the Golden State, and as we all know, Los Angeles is the Golden City of the Golden State. The San Luis Rey tribe called what is now Pasadena, "place of the poppies." Spanish Californians called the poppy *dormi dera*—the drowsy one—because its petals curl up at night.

In spring the 1800-acre preserve in blanketed with orange, yellow and golden poppies—an incredible sight. From the Visitor Center our 3.3 mile hike along the Antelope loop trail leads up an easy meandering grade to Kitanemuk Vista at an elevation of nearly 3000 feet. The elevation gain to Antelope Butte is about 300 feet. From the vista point, trails wander in all directions and your hike can be customized with added miles. Before you set off, however, take in the view. Besides the endless carpets of poppies, the rugged Tehachapis are to the north, Mojave Desert is east, Sierra Pelonas to the south and Gormon Hills are west. It's captivating scenery.

Bring sunglasses, sunscreen and hat even when it's cold or cloudy. The preserve literally offers no shade.

Prance along the trails and feel like a kid in Wonderland. Customize your hike or return to the

Visitor Center from the Kitanemuk Vista along the loop trail.

In order to keep the fields in a strictly natural and pristine state, the park service does not water or stimulate the flowers. This show is all nature at work. Sheep and cattle grazing on hillsides is not allowed and the rules strictly enforced. With the exception of service dogs, pets are prohibited. Stay on the trails and DO NOT PICK THE FLOWERS.

Time your visit so you can attend the California Poppy Festival in April in the city of Lancaster, east of the preserve. It's a hoot! Flowers at the festival include lupine, clover and cream cups—but the poppy is king.

My next recommendation may border on sacrilege. Since the poppies only bloom during the spring, naturally that's when the crowds are present. Try a trip to the preserve in fall or winter. True, no poppies, but the enormous Antelope Butte is still there and I guarantee no one else will be. The views from Kitanemuk Vista remain the same and are fascinating, and there is something bewitching about the brown barren bluffs. Enjoy.

Side trip – Take a short drive, about seven miles west on Lancaster Road, to Arthur B. Ripley Desert Woodland State Park. This is a ghost park, meaning no one ever visits. The small isolated 506-acre park is a tiny slice of heaven and has an extraordinary grove of Joshua trees. These stately beauties were once in great abundance in Antelope Valley, but have fallen victim to farming, ranching and housing expansion. The Joshua tree was named by Mormon pioneers who saw the tree with its upraised arms as the prophet Joshua leading the Israelites to the Promised Land. Actually, the tree is a member of the lily family with a white bloom in spring. Arthur B. Ripley Desert Woodland State Park is much lusher than Saddleback Butte State Park, with plenty of junipers. Its short and self-guided nature trail is lonely and exquisite.

Hike # 5

Placerita Canyon County Park

"You can't beat L.A.'s weather and scenery. Isn't it worth it to adjust to whatever annoys you to be able to live 365 days a year instead of hibernating November thru April? NYC may have culture, but it's also dirty, crowded and everyone is in a bad mood all the time."
- Grateful Deb

Directions – From the San Fernando Valley, take the 405 north to Highway 14 (Antelope Valley Freeway). In 2.6 miles take Exit 3, Placerita Canyon Road. Turn right (south) and in 1.5 miles look for signs to the park entrance on the right (west).

Placerita Canyon County Park is a 1351-acre (not including the upper trails) jewel of a park less than a 20-minute drive from the San Fernando Valley. It boasts an excellent visitor center, a soothing river trail with awesome oak hammocks, a waterfall trail and a steep and rugged loop trail that leads to a remote ridge overlooking the North Valley Conservation Preserve and hills above the town of Sylmar, epicenter of the 1971 earthquake.

Six years before gold was discovered at Sutter's Mill near Sacramento, initiating the 1849 California Gold Rush, the first documented discovery of gold in Mexico's upper or Alta California (lower California is Baja) occurred in Placerita Canyon on March 9, 1842. At Rancho San Francisco, Francisco Lopez took a nap under a huge oak tree now known as the Oak of the Golden Dream. Speaking of dreams, Lopez reportedly had a whopper, dreaming he was floating along a river of gold. When he awoke, he was famished, so he dug up some wild onions for a sandwich. Flakes of gold and whole nuggets clung to the onion's roots. The minor gold rush spurred by Lopez' discovery quickly petered out. Today, the Oak of the Golden Dream is a California State Historical Landmark.

Speaking of history, Theodore (he hated being called Teddy) Roosevelt hunted up Placerita Canyon in the late 1890s with pal "Rosey" Melrose, who had earlier gunned down the mayor of Acton, D.M. Broom, in a raucous wild west gun fight. Rosey was a hair faster. He was not only acquitted of all charges, but he later helped nominate Roosevelt for president.

Remnants of the historic Walker Ranch and cabin, built in 1920 by Frank Walker, are still on the grounds, and scores of old TV westerns and movies were filmed on location, including *Hopalong Cassidy* and *The Cisco Kid.* At one time or another John Wayne, Tim Holt and Roy Rodgers, among others, rode roughshod throughout the Walker Ranch.

The park contains a complex flora system with live oaks, willows, cottonwoods and California sycamores dotting the landscape. Many are impressively large specimens. The outstanding visitor center has live animals on display, including several species of hawk.

Naturally, ghosts inhabit Placerita Canyon. After a disastrous flood in 1928 washed out a cemetery and set the spirits loose, numerous misty spectral images have been reported throughout the canyon. Once, a rancher was painting his barn in the early evening. He stopped to wipe his brow and look at the sunset. When he glanced back at the wall, dozens of wet palm prints were in the paint. Also, in 1974-75, heiress Patricia Hearst was reputedly stashed in one of the cabins up the canyon as a captive of the Symbionese Liberation Army during one of America's largest manhunts. Numerous sightings of the pretty granddaughter of William Randolph Hearst were reported to local officials.

For our first hike, take the short 300-yard trail north, under the highway, to the Oak of the Golden Dream. It's still flourishing and much bigger than when Francisco Lopez took his nap in 1842. You gotta see this baby, but don't go looking for gold among the wild onions. Then, retrace your steps and hike south on the 2.1-mile round trip Placerita Creek trail to the center of Walker Ranch. If the creek is rushing, this is one of the finest and most majestic creek trails in Southern California. Huge oaks, cottonwoods and grassy banks line the trail, with dozens of gorgeous resting sites begging you to stop, linger and enjoy an adult beverage (which is probably prohibited within the park boundaries, so be discreet). At times the creek can be low, slow or even dry. Spring is an opportunistic time for rushing water. A local yarn claims UFOs take the water for their spaceship crews.

At Walker Ranch, the 0.5 waterfall trail is a huge disappointment. I've visited the trail three times and still can't reliably pinpoint where the heck the falls are located, unless it's along a small slippery slope of rock where I've seen a dribble of water. Forget the waterfall and take the picturesque Los Pinetos Trail to the top of Santa Clarita ridge. The trail is uphill but manageable and worth it—the woods are filled with California Walnut trees and you could fill your daypack if you're lucky. You'll also pass Pinetos Springs, which is a reliable source of potable water. At the top of the ridge, look to the west for Mission Peak and its forested ridges, or south toward the town of Sylmar. Return to your car on the same route.

Hike # 6

Strawberry Peak

"I grew up in utopia, I did. Los Angeles, when I was a child, was paradise."
— Larry G.

Directions – Take La Canada exit off I-210 and drive 14 miles east on the Angeles Crest Highway (2) to Red Box Gap parking area and follow trail signs across the highway.

At 6167 feet, Strawberry Peak is the highest mountain in the frontal range of the San Gabriel Mountains facing Los Angeles. Translated, that means it has the finest view of L.A.'s downtown skyline as well as the Palos Verde Peninsula, Pacific Ocean and Santa Catalina Island—on a clear day.

The hike is 6.6 miles round trip and the final mile to the peak is a heart-pounding ascent that is truly satisfying. Don't be fooled by the two false summits. Continue along the ridgeline to the actual peak, which should be obvious.

Strawberry Peak was named in the early 1900s by mountain climbers training for the Swiss Alps who thought the mountain resembled a huge upside-down strawberry. Coloring did not factor into the equation.

My brother Chris and I attempted to tilt our heads in order to understand the climbers' logic, but with no success. I consider myself to be an imaginative guy, but have no clue what those guys had been ingesting. Chris and I thought the upside-down peak looked like a giant dry martini—shaken not stirred.

A scary urban legend associated with Strawberry Peak has lingered for years. Many demonologists (is that an actual career choice?) believe there is a haunted body-dump for the unfortunate victims of devil sacrifices on the mountain's slopes. L.A. has a unique history with Satanism and the occult. It certainly didn't harm the spooky myth when an actual L.A. deputy sheriff was quoted once as saying, "If I yelled out for every dead person buried up there to stand up, it would look like Venice Beach on a Sunday." Yikes!

From Red Box Gap parking lot, cross the highway and climb 0.6 miles up to a series of switchbacks. I labeled the switchbacks "flats" because they were considerably less steep than the first 0.6 miles. My brother failed to see any humor in my description, since the switchbacks do have a noticeable incline and are completely in the sun. Beware: it's a rocky and slippery trail.

At 2.2 miles from Red Box Gap you'll reach a saddle and a signed fork. Turn left (north) and begin an earnest 1.1-mile ascent that includes some steep rock climbing to the peak. Take your time; I always say life is not a supposed to be a day at the gym—hiking is for enjoyment. The climb is more difficult and longer than it looks. On websites, many hikers speak of a "serious butt-kicking," so be prepared. Shortness is your only comfort.

On Strawberry Peak's craggy summit you'll be rewarded with shade and grass to lounge away the afternoon while leaning against one of the trunks of scattered bigcone Douglas fir or Coulter pine. I still recommend not sitting or standing under a Coulter pine—no need to take a chance of getting bonked on the head by one of the tree's cannon ball cones. Sit near a snow patch in order to cool your beer or wine bottle. Some hikers claim the views of the L.A. basin are superior on one of the mountains closer to town. What planet are they from? Strawberry Peak's immaculate vistas are incomparable, and the clean fresh air is invigorating and intoxicating. Gaze at the Pacific Ocean, identify the downtown skyscrapers or search the sky for golden eagles.

Incidentally, every publication about this hike claims that rattlesnakes are a danger. Those publications are fear mongers and alarmists. Ophidiophobes! Even if rattlesnakes are common, it'd still be rare to see one. I've made three trips up Strawberry Peak, two in summer, and have yet to see a rattlesnake. This fear and loathing of rattlesnakes is silly and has got to stop. Rattlesnakes are shy and non-aggressive, rattle loudly if distressed, and will do practically anything to get away from humans. Most snake bites occur when people tease or attempt to kill or capture a snake. Leave them alone and you'll be safe. If you see any type of snake, back away and the world will be a better place.

Reminder: the 6.6 miles has little shade. Bring hat, sunscreen and sunglasses. Leave the dorky hiking poles at home. God, I hate those things. Besides being obnoxious and doofy, they won't help a bit on the 1.1-mile climb to the peak. Return to your car on the same route.

Sidenote - I have a vision: Let's establish National Park status for a large chunk of the San Gabriel Mountains, including Strawberry Peak, all within the boundaries of the Angeles National Forest. Not the entire forest, just a select swath along the Angeles Crest. There's already something called the San Gabriel Mountains National Monument, though it appears the government is trying to keep it a secret, so let's upgrade. Keep other sections open for hunting, skiing and ATVs. Stretch the new park's boundaries from Strawberry Peak to Mts. Gleason, Pacifico, Hillyer and Baden-Powell, and include Chilo and Charlton Flats, and Devil's Canyon Wilderness.

Why? Why not?

1) The area needs more protection and cash pumped into its operations. 19 million people live nearby and that causes a variety of wear and tear.

2) It'll add status and revenues for maintenance, upgrades and law enforcement.
3) It will limit and control overuse.

Think about it. San Gabriel Mountains National Park—a national park with sensational trails, campgrounds and fishing—all within view of downtown Los Angeles. It could become the City of Angels personal recreational playground.

Hike # 7

Mt. Baden-Powell

"The only angels in Los Angeles are in Heaven and they're looking down on the Dodgers."
— Tommy Lasorda

Directions – Take La Canada exit off I-210 and drive 50 miles east on the Angeles Crest Highway (2) to Vincent Gap parking area. Follow signs to trailhead.

Baron Robert Baden-Powell, who liked to be called Lord or BP, was a Lt. General in the British army and saw extensive action during World War I. He was also the founder and first chief scout of the International Boy Scouts in 1909.

"I believe God put us in this jolly world to be happy and enjoy life," he said.

Jolly good! Sounds like an excellent philosophy for hikers.

Lord Baden-Powell was an elegant gentleman, fond of wearing a Stetson, red neckerchief and his military medals. He was regarded as an incredible teller of "ripping yarns," which would certainly make for a perfect campfire counselor. He died January 8, 1941.

His gravestone at St. Peter's cemetery in Nyeri, Kenya bears a circle with a dot in the center, which is the trail sign for "going home."

The 9407-foot Mt. Baden-Powell, also known as East Twin or Little Baldy, is a worthy mountain to be named for such a worthy gentleman. It was christened by the United States Geological Survey agency at a dedication ceremony in 1931. The famed 53-mile-long Silver Moccasin Trail ends on the summit. To this day boy scouts hike the trail for a merit badge. The hike to the peak is 8 miles round trip with a challenging ascent that has forty switchbacks, count 'em, and an elevation gain of 2818 feet.

There's not much flat ground on this hike, but early on you'll enjoy hiking through a lovely shaded grove of pines. One mile up is a bench with views of the eastern peaks. At 1.7 miles, look for the knotted tree, a well-known and popular landmark. Be careful on the ridgeline; it's not really dangerous, but patches of slippery snow may be encountered, even in summer, and powerful winds that have gnarled the trees could have you swaying back and forth. Remember: when hiking in the wilderness, it is your responsibility not to get hurt or do something stupid. You could endanger members of your party or would-be rescuers. The phrase, "Here, hold my beer," should not apply in the wilderness.

At 3.5 miles a short unmarked 0.2-mile spur trail leads to an ancient grove of limber pines, similar to bristlecone. Many of these specimens are over two thousand years old, rivaling the longevity of most sequoias. Also, you'll encounter incomparable views of the upper Mojave Desert, Devil's Punchbowl, Pine Mountain and Mt. Baldy. There are few better views on any mountain in Southern California.

Cross the Pacific Crest National Trail and continue towards the peak. Be sure to check out the "Wally Waldron" tree, named after a popular Boy Scout counselor. It's a fine example of a mature limber pine and believed to be the oldest living thing in the San Gabriel Mountains.

You are now only 0.1 mile from the summit and concrete marker to Lord BP himself. At the top, relax and sip an adult beverage. Be proud of your accomplishment. Revel in the breathtaking views and incredibly blue sky that appears to be dripping with Salvador Dali-style white clouds. Naturally, the spirit of Lord Baden-Powell reportedly resides on the peak.

"No one can pass through life, any more than he can pass through a bit of country, without leaving tracks behind, and those tracks may often be helpful to those coming after him in finding their own way."
- Lord Robert Baden-Powell

Hike # 8

Mt. Hillyer

*"L.A. will do you so wrong,
and then do you so right."*
- B.B. King

Directions – Take La Canada exit off I-210 and drive 28 miles east on the Angeles Crest Highway (2) to Santa Clara Divide Road. Turn left (north). Drive 2.3 miles and take a left on Campground Road. Follow signs to Horse Flats Campground.

Horse Flats Campground is usually a serene and idyllic spot. I'm certain it has its mob weekends, but during weekdays or off-season few people will be there. It has 26 shaded campsites for $12 a night and, of course, horse corrals. At 5650 feet elevation it is cooler than the basin or Valley in summer, with pleasant night air spiced with sage and incense cedar. The campground was a former horse thief hideout at the turn of the century.

Unfortunately, federal money is needed to spruce up the place. Not just at Horse Flats, but at Chilo, Charlton Flats and Cooper Creek. At one time, these recreation areas were state-of-the-art, and the fact that they have become dilapidated because of funding shortfalls is nothing less than shameful. These four recreation areas could be centerpieces for the new San Gabriel Mountains National Park. If the United States federal government can dole out rich corporate subsidies and welfare to big oil, lumber, gas, mining, ranching and agriculture—how about properly funding our National Parks and Forests? In fact, the mammoth industries that benefit directly from the tax breaks and subsidies should contribute to a fund to do just that! If these corporations would willingly donate generous amounts to a park fund, they might find themselves with a lot more friends instead of incurring upon themselves the wrath of environmental advocates. Our park services and rangers deserve better. Allocate adequate funding so that staff can perform their jobs and maintain our natural habitats.

End of rant.

At Horse Flats campground, gaze west across the open area toward the slopes of boulder-strewn Mt. Hillyer. The top is your destination. This was bandit and horse thief country so beware. The hike to the summit is only a 4.0-mile round trip, but it appears longer and the ascent isn't easy. I have you skipping the Silver Moccasin Trail out of Chilo because it is uninteresting, has no shade, and is usually loaded with mentally defective mountain bikers. These inconsiderate boobs are supposed to give way to hikers and horses, but rarely do. Large contingents will barrel down the trail, yelling their fool heads off for you to leap out of their way. Please refrain from knocking them on their asses.

To start your hike, cross the large open flat to the west and begin your steady ascent among a maze of boulders. It's nearly impossible to get lost, but easy to wander off the trail. Pay attention. On the way up you probably won't see any bandits, but there are plenty of inviting rocks to scramble up for expansive and breathtaking views. Try a few. Mt. Baldy is just one of the many peaks lingering in the distance.

This is bear and mountain lion country. Stay alert.

Rock scrambling during the ascent may be the highlight of your hike. The aromatic fragrance of sage, chaparral and cedar will heighten your senses. As you near the summit, don't look for a peak or marker. You'll be heading into stately sugar, Jeffrey and Coulter pines as well as bigcone Douglas fir. Steady breezes will sway the tree limbs and fan the air with the scent of pine. Few things will soothe the mind better than the smell of pine or sound of wind rustling through their glistening needles. I need a nap!

Near the summit are outstanding views of Twin Peak (I want some cherry pie), Mt. Waterman and Mt. Baldy. The top of Mt. Hillyer is a sprawling hump of forest rather than a craggy peak. For mountain baggers, the summit shows itself slightly along the western ridge. Every trail publication appears to mock the top of Mt. Hillyer because of its lack of views. Like what Gertrude Stein said of Oakland, one guide claimed,

"There is no there there." So what? If you want a view, drive up to the top of nearby Pacifico Mountain. I love the top of Mt. Hillyer because you will not find a more peaceful or attractive spot in the Angeles National Forest. You can still get a view if you explore the edges of the mountain. Me? I'm satisfied to park my butt in the center of the forest and relax. The top is a secluded refuge of dense pine and cool fresh air. Silence—except for the wind in the trees and an occasional scream from a hawk or raven. This is a place to read, write, converse, recoup, meditate and enjoy an adult beverage. Spend an afternoon on top of Mt. Hillyer and I guarantee you won't regret it. Remember: you're barely fifteen miles, as the crow flies, from the L.A basin and 19 million people.

Most trail guides recommend you continue hiking north off the peak and hook up with a forest road for your trip back to Horse Flats. Balderdash! Who wants to hike on a dusty dirt road filled with ATV lunatics zooming by? I'm a big fan of round trips. You may be on the same trail, but you're going in the opposite direction, so it will appear almost new.

Hike # 9

Devil's Canyon

"These days, the City of Angels wasn't the easygoing place it had once been – and the hope of actually finding anyone living even an approximation of an angelic existence was slim indeed. Devils, yes. Those were relatively simple to locate."
- Dean Koontz

Directions – Take La Canada exit off I-210 and drive 27 miles east on the Angeles Crest Highway (2). Trailhead is on right (south) side of road with a small parking area on the left (north) side.

Devil's Canyon Trail goes through the heart of the 36,118-acre San Gabriel Wilderness area, established in 1968, making it one of the first wilderness areas in the nation. Unfortunately, the colossal Station Fire of 2009 (ignited by arsonists) burned trees along slopes that now allow rains to slick up the trail, but much of the canyon remains intact. Devil's Canyon is a special place to the city of Los Angeles. No other metropolis has a designated wilderness area practically next door to its downtown area, only 18 miles as the golden eagle flies. When you're submerged in the canyon, the city seems hundreds of miles away.

Prior to starting your hike, stand at the trailhead on the Angeles Crest Highway and gaze into the wilderness area below you. Talk about photo opportunities! Devil's Canyon is spectacular, and I assure you most visitors simply gawk at the view from this spot, snap a few pictures and load back up in their tour bus or car and continue on to Wrightwood. You and I will head down the trail. Devil's Canyon will wrap its arms around a hiker, and it certainly feels good to be hugged by a wilderness.

Careful: beware of poodle-dog bush, a vicious skin irritant that is not very well-known. I know, it's not easy to take a plant called poodle-dog bush seriously, but the stuff can be nasty on the skin, much like poison ivy or oak. This is why when I hike an area like Devil's Canyon I don't wear shorts or even short-sleeves. I want the protection of jeans from scrapes, scratches, bugs and poisonous plants. My rule on the trail is that if you can't identify it, don't touch it!

Please bring the pooch—it's a wilderness area and no leash law applies.

If you hike in spring or early summer, Indian paintbrush, baby blue eyes and western wildflowers are blooming, and they attract butterflies. Plus, the stream should be rushing boldly.

Devil's Canyon Trail is a seven-mile round trip with a 1500-foot elevation drop on a series of well-designed switchbacks. I say well-designed because, though a 1500 foot climb out may seem daunting, it really isn't too difficult of an ascent if you take your time. Just note: it's all downhill going in and all uphill coming out.

I've done this hike twice, both times in early June, and there's always been sufficient water in the creek. In fact I've discovered a perfect 3-4 foot deep dipping hole along the creek that is splendid to sit in, relax and cool down. It's easy to dunk your head. But many publications complain about low or even no water, so be forewarned. Late summer is probably a bad time for a visit. Also, the trail is a bit more rugged than most—watch your footing.

The canyon is secluded, remote and lush. After 2.0 miles, the trail picks up the creek and things really start to get interesting. Several crossings will occur. Also, the deeper into the canyon you venture, the more heavily forested the terrain becomes.

At 3.5 miles the trail peters out at a primitive backpacking campsite directly on the creek. No signs, benches or tables—only a fire pit. You may encounter nudists! The location appears to be a favorite hangout for the *au natural* gang. I don't mind nudists. My only problem is that many nudists are people no one wants to see nude. Now if *Sports Illustrated* sponsored a swimsuit issue party in the canyon that'd be different. Many nudists need to look in the mirror. I'm at the age where I feel sheepish about taking my shirt off, let alone everything else. But if the nudists don't mind, I suppose I can handle it.

I've heard many tales about a legendary waterfall about two miles further downstream. I even forged on once for about 0.5 miles. It was a little tough. You have to boulder hop, wade, and bushwhack to reach your goal. I don't recommend it. Poison oak, ticks, rattlesnakes, injury or death await the bold, fearless and foolish. Of all the hikers who have told me about the waterfall, none have actually hiked to it.

Take it slow and easy on your hike back out.

Hike # 10

Cooper Creek Falls

"Sometimes being alone is all we need."
- Charles Bukowski

Directions – Take the La Canada exit off I-210 and drive 35 miles east on the Angeles Crest Highway (2). Just past Mt. Waterman ski area turn left (north) into Buckhorn campground. It's 0.4 miles to trailhead. Follow signs.

Our round trip hike to Cooper Falls is a tad over 3 miles with a 700-foot elevation drop. Once again, that means 700 feet back up on the way out, so conserve your energy. The trail is gradual and not difficult. Your quest is a cool and relaxing waterfall that cascades down a mossy cliff year round.

The hike to the falls is in a shady canyon with rare old growth forest that includes ponderosa pine, alder and oak. Believe it or not, a few decent-sized redwoods line the trail. During the final 0.5 miles you'll hear a babbling brook at the bottom of the canyon. For much of the hike you'll be following the Burkhart Trail. Yes, it's the same trail that traverses all the way to Devil's Punchbowl.

Oh, I forgot. At the trailhead for Cooper Creek an Adventure Pass is required on your dashboard. In fact, you'll need one for Strawberry Peak, Mts. Hillyer and Baden-Powell and Devil's Canyon too. It's a $5 fee to park anywhere in the Angeles National Forest, even on the side of any road. Of all the inane, gimmicky stunts to extort money from the public, the Adventure Pass stands out as the biggest rip-off. If you park on the side of a road to read a sign, enjoy the view, switch drivers or take a leak—you need an Adventure Pass. Park at any picnic site or trailhead—you need an Adventure Pass. And so on. I'd like to see how the hunters, ATVers and horseback riders up in Montana would handle the Adventure Pass. The federal government is simply stealing money from the residents of Los Angeles and San Diego.

I don't mind paying legitimate fees to the Forest Service, hopefully it helps, but the Adventure Pass is silly and certainly would not be tolerated in other national forests. Plus, the pass is nearly impossible to purchase on a weekday. On weekends, rangers will man portable booths on the Angeles Crest Highway to sell the passes, but not on weekdays. I tried to buy a pass at a ranger station in the Angeles National Forest on a weekday but the office was closed. No self-service boxes either. On their website, the forest service has a list of vendors outside the forests that will sell an Adventure Pass. I kid you not; in Palmdale you can buy a pass at 4 Points Liquor store and in Santa Ynez, the Second Amendment Gun shop. This takes way too much planning and is totally impractical. I doubt you'd want to send your teenager into a liquor store or gun shop to buy a pass. Ridiculous! After I got ticketed for not having an Adventure Pass, I started leaving $5 under my windshield wiper. No one ever touched it. Also, there are 154 national forests in America and only four require the pass. Yep, you guessed it—all four are in Southern California (Angeles, Los Padres, Cleveland and San Bernardino). What the - ?

My question is: does the money benefit just those four national forests (like it should) or does it go into a general kitty? A recent court case ruled against the Adventure Pass and forest officials howled in protest. I am somewhat sympathetic. Since we all pay taxes, why don't the politicians delegate sufficient funding for our natural wonders? It's not the responsibility of hikers to pay all the costs. All Americans should pay—even if they don't visit the parks. You live in America, don't you? Our national forests and parks are national treasures and to maintain them adequately says a lot about who we are as a society and what we value. It's like public schools; everyone should pay for them whether or not you have a child in the system. Public schools are the future of our nation. What selfish miser doesn't believe in paying for American children's education? Likewise with national parks and forests. The forest service maintains and defends our national landscape. They deserve proper and adequate funding. As said before, many corporations reap the benefits of our national forests for pennies on the dollar. They should pay their fair share. An Adventure Pass would be much more palatable if they were required in all national forests, made easier to purchase and the collected monies could be used only to fund the national forests.

Okay, I'll stop.

Back to Cooper Creek Falls trail. After 1.5 miles, a short but steep spur trail, with ropes to aid your descent and ascent, leads to the creek and falls. Enchanting! The granite wall is over thirty feet high and water runs down the mossy face year round. It's gorgeous and the creek has trout swimming in its pools. Also, the creek is excellent for wading. Several large boulders make the perfect spot to for relaxing and viewing. You will be charmed and seduced. Cooper Falls is a must hike for all Angelinos.

Following your visit to the falls, continue south on the main trail to the top of Pleasant View Ridge. It will add an additional 3.0 miles, but it is very much worth it. The remoteness and incredible views are glorious, and you'll have to remind yourself that about 20 miles southwest is the L.A. Civic Center. Unfortunately, much of the forest along the ridge was destroyed by the 2009 Station Fire, which was the largest forest fire in L.A. County history and ignited by arsonists. What is it with maniacs and fire? Didn't your mother teach you not to play with matches? The fire killed two courageous firefighters, so add homicide to the arson charge, you pyro-creeps! Maybe we should bring back burning at the stake.

Hike # 11

Halfmoon Campground

*"No second chances in the valley
of ten million insanities."*
— Ry Cooder

Directions – Take I-5 north from the San Fernando Valley and drive 74 miles. Exit at Frazier Mountain Highway. Turn left (west) and drive through the towns of Frazier Park and Lake of the Woods. Continue 15 miles west on Lockwood Valley Road. Turn left at Grade Valley-Mutau Flat Road (FR # 7NO3) and continue south 9 miles to Halfmoon Campground at the FR 7N13 junction.

You're probably wondering why I'm including a campground as one of our hikes, but this campground is 9 miles deep inside a remote and radiant wilderness that can serve as a base camp for a dozen or more separate hikes or bushwhacks. It's well off the beaten path. In fact, the drive to the campground is part of the adventure. Access off Lockwood Valley road is a long dirt road that includes a climb over a forested ridge with several creek crossings that will discourage most drivers. A high clearance vehicle is recommended. I've done the drive in a Jeep Liberty and Nissan Exterra with no trouble. Halfmoon Campground is secluded and lovely, and the road runs parallel to Piru Creek for much of the way. RVs, trailers and low-level sedans are not advisable.

Halfmoon Campground is also adjacent to Piru Creek and at 4700-foot elevation it sits among stately ponderosa pines. It has only 12 campsites, on a first come-first serve basis. This is a spectacular spot to relax and/or set up for hikes and mountain bike treks. FR 7N13 continues SE for miles and is great for exploring. The dirt road is solitary and desolate. Wander off the road and do a little bushwhacking. The entire area feels like a boundless wilderness.

Set up chairs and relax by Piru Creek with its year-round running water. Signs inform that an Adventure Pass is required. Oh, for the love of— .

For the hiker, Halfmoon Campground is a doorway to a bushwhacking mecca. By bushwhacking, I simply mean hiking without a trail, not hacking through chaparral and briars with a machete. A compass and a good sense of direction are nice, but the road and campground are visible from nearly all the ridges and ravines. The hiking is not treacherous and it would be difficult to become lost.

My recommendation: lock up your vehicle and hike south to Piru Creek. Ford the creek and choose one of the many slopes or gullies between the ridges to begin a hike. Wend your way through the forest and hike as far and high up as you please. Opportunities are limitless. Swoop down into a gully and climb a different ridge. This is mountain hiking and exploring at its finest. Enjoy the magnificent views of the valley that you just drove across, and awesome peaks in the distance. This could be a mystical experience along with the ultimate freedom. You're on your own to choose any direction to hike. Take your time to savor and enjoy the experience. Freedom is what Angelinos are all about and this area offers hiking independence. Bushwhacking through the pine scented mountains surrounding Los Angeles is my favorite form of hiking, and many of the hikes described in this book can be altered into satisfying bushwhack adventures.

On my most recent journey to Halfmoon Campground, I rested on a small remote peak with an awesome view of the creek, camping area and valley. Then I noticed I could zip down a small cut and climb farther to a higher, heavily forested ridge. I could see that it was a special spot with several large specimens of Jeffrey pine as well as a perfect place to enjoy an adult beverage. But I had already hiked nearly three miles up and the sun hung low in the western sky. I decide to save that spot for my next visit.

After your return trip to the campground, light a small fire in one of the fire pits. Bring hot dogs, hamburger or steaks for the grill and watch the moon rise in the east. If you drive out in the dark, you may see loads of wildlife alongside of the road.

Stop at the truck stop at I-5 off Frazier Mountain Highway and buy some coffee for the trip home.

Hike # 12

Dome Springs

"Los Angeles is a funhouse mirror offering grotesque, exaggerated reflections of America itself."
— David L. Ulin

Directions – Take I-5 north from the San Fernando Valley and drive 74 miles. Exit at Frazier Mountain Highway. Turn left (west) and drive through the towns of Frazier Park and Lake of the Woods. Continue 10 miles west on Lockwood Valley Road. Turn right (north) on FR 8N40. Go 3 bumpy miles to a primitive campground.

Our hike into Dome Springs is another freewheeling bushwhacking affair into a mystical land of hoodoos, mesas and dried creek beds. Hike as far as you care in nearly any direction. The dried creek beds help form a huge and complex maze, and serve as excellent avenues into this magical world. Ponderosa, Jeffrey and pinyon pines cluster at the top of many small mesas. The area is rugged and certainly not for sandals.

Dome Springs Campground has only a few barely defined sites with tables and fire rings. However, it is a great base for robust hikes into an austere wilderness. Several hoodoos and pinnacles invite the climber to scramble to the top for incredible views of Lockwood Valley and the SE slopes of Mt. Pinos. After your hike, you can settle into one of the campsites for a grilled supper and adult beverage. More than likely, you'll find yourself alone.

Dome Springs is a remote and isolated area that sits in the shadow of Mt. Pinos. At 8831 feet, Pinos is the highest mountain in the Los Padres National Forest. This is badlands territory with extra-large pinyon pines, manzanitas and even sturdy yuccas. Be careful and alert, and do not underestimate the possibility of hazards in such a harsh wilderness. At 4800-5500 feet elevation, the area can be delightfully cool in fall, winter and spring. Summer, on the other hand, can be blazingly hot.

Bear, bobcat, mule deer, coyote, fox and mountain lion haunt the maze. I've seen loads of bear tracks in the dried creek beds. Also, you can access the Chumash Wilderness for longer treks or backpack hikes.

Speaking of the maze that is formed by creek beds, my brother Chris and I spent an afternoon hiking and crawling up a few of the smaller avenues. Whenever we took a short break, the silence was almost piercing. As we worked our way back to the campground, a full moon hung low over the ponderosa pines to the east. We reached a fork and—Holy Cow, Batman—bumped into two other hikers. We all yelped in unison, and then laughed our asses off.

Speaking of climbs, my wife Elaine and I scrambled to the top of a crusty hoodoo and tight roped across its upper ridge. Instead of going down on the same path we came up, we decided to slide down a different and steeper slope. Bad move! About halfway down we got swept up by loose gravel and sand that threatened to start an avalanche. Going back up would have been a hand-over-hand crawl, while continuing down could have turned into a 200-foot somersault. We decided to sit on our butts and slide down cautiously in single file with me in the lead. We made it, but not without some thrills and surly grumbling.

My hiking recommendation is to boldly push north up the main and largest dried creek bed, and explore at will. Stop frequently to take your bearings, enjoy the scenery and plot your route. Dozens of offshoots and possibilities will appear. Climb a mesa for a snack and overview, and then dive back into the maze for more hiking. It would be difficult to get lost because of the obvious direction of the creeks and position of the sun, but always be mindful of your location and surroundings. Using a compass can help and does not make you a wuss. In warmer weather, keep an eye out for rattlesnakes. Wander to your heart's content.

Rejoice in the secluded nature of the Dome Springs maze. This is reputed to have been bandit country in the mid to later 1800s. Keep an eye out for Joaquin Murrieta.

Hike # 13

Mt. Pinos

"See, that's the thing about Los Angeles, when you've mastered the art of feeling lonely in a room full of people, that's when you know."
- Kris Kidd

Directions – Take I-5 north from the San Fernando Valley and drive 74 miles. Exit at Frazier Mountain Highway. Turn left (west) and drive 7.2 miles to the hamlet of Lake of the Woods. Veer right onto Cuddy Valley Road and drive 22.5 miles to the paved parking lot on top of Mt. Pinos. Gate to the trail is on the left (west) side of parking lot.

This is my favorite hike.

At 8831 feet, Mt. Pinos is the highest mountain in Ventura County while Sawmill Mountain (just one gap to the west) at 8818 feet is the highest point in Kern County. Mt. Pinos is also considered the finest site for astronomy viewing and stargazing in Southern California that is accessible by car. Dry mountain air, altitude and lack of city lights make for perfect conditions. The parking area, along with adjacent Chula Vista walk-in campground, are favorite gathering places for amateur and professional astronomers who own expensive telescopes and will happily offer hikers a peek into the solar system and Milky Way.

Pass through the gate on the west side of the parking lot and hike a rolling 1.5 miles to the summit of Mt. Pinos. Historically, this was the premier observation site for the rare California condor. Numbers, however, became so low that conservationists initiated a daring program to capture all of the remaining birds in the wild and begin a captive breeding program. Amazingly, the plan was successful and scores of condors have been released back into the wild at several locations, including Mt. Pinos and Grand Canyon. Condors are majestic and spectacular, boasting 8-12 foot wingspans, orange heads and a white vee under each wing.

Also, along the 1.5-mile hike to the peak, you'll pass through an amazing old-growth forest of ponderosa and Jeffrey pine, with many of the specimens being huge. Stick your nose inside the bark and sniff the aromas of vanilla, pineapple and butterscotch.

From the information sign at the peak of Mt. Pinos, take the Vincent Tumamait Trail northwest and descend on a series of switchbacks to the gap between Mt. Pinos and Sawmill Mountain. Vincent Tumamait was a Chumash Native American elder and spiritual leader who helped create a renaissance of Chumash culture in the mid-20th century. He was born in 1919 and died at the age of 73 on August 12, 1992.

Mt. Pinos is at the edge of the 38,150-acre Chumash Wilderness Area; you'll pass a sign on your descent off Mt. Pinos. At the gap, or saddle, you'll be at 8320 feet elevation. I haven't seen many large animals (bear, deer, etc.) in this area, but they're out here. Once, at the saddle, I heard a piercing feline scream and found tracks in the snow. I was fairly certain it was a bobcat, not a mountain lion, but I never sighted the provocative little kitty.

This is also bandit country. Legendary bandits Joaquin Murrieta and Three-Fingered Jack used what are now Sheep Campground and the surrounding area, including Dome Springs, as hideouts.

From the saddle, climb up to where the trail starts to level off and delight in the spectacle of a captivating grove of old-growth Jeffrey pine, many of them severely stunted from decades of howling wind. It's a magical place that has become my favorite wilderness spot around the Los Angeles region. Joaquin Murrieta would definitely approve. In fact, I'm certain Murrieta wandered past these trees many times.

Bushwhack north to the top of Sawmill Ridge. Locate the large stone kiosk that marks the summit of Sawmill Mountain and look west. The views are superb, but don't stop there. Look northeast; about 0.7 of a mile further out is "the Point." Hike east along the faint trail, avoiding a sharp gully, and then make a beeline to "the Point." Now the views of Mt. Abel and the San Joaquin Valley are incomparable.

Back on the main trail, hike west for 0.5 miles to a short spur trail to Sheep Campground. It's another 0.4 miles to the site. Sheep Campground is a pleasant picnic spot unless the Boy Scouts have invaded and are whooping it up.

Return to your car on the same route for a total of 5-6 miles.

Sidenote - Chula Vista walk-in Campground, on the east side of the parking lot on top of Mt. Pinos, is an excellent gateway for exploring the eastern half of this rounded mountain. It's also a nice picnic spot. You can easily bushwhack to several remote and secluded vistas. Also, a few miles back down the road, look for McGill Campground and park at the McGill trailhead. It's a 4.0-mile hike to the highway below, mostly downhill. Hike in for a mile or so just for a quick taste.

Hike # 14

Sawmill Mountain

"A short drive from L.A. will take you up into high mountains with cold blue lakes, or out over the Mojave Desert, with its weird vegetation and immense vistas, or smack into the face of the Pacific Ocean. Accept it, and you'll be happy."
                          - Christopher Isherwood

Directions – Take I-5 north from the San Fernando Valley and drive 14 miles. Exit at Lake Hughes Road. Drive 23 miles northeast and turn left (NW) at CR N2 or Elizabeth Lake Road. Drive 4.56 miles to the unsigned trailhead on the left (south) side of the highway. Park and look west—trail will be obvious.

This Sawmill Mountain is in the Liebre Mountains of the northern Angeles National Forest and not the same Sawmill Mountain that is shouldering Mt. Pinos.
    Our hike takes us up Shake Canyon and through Upper Shake Canyon Campground to a spur trail that leads to a 2.0-mile stretch of the Pacific Crest Trail along the top of Sawmill ridge in the Liebre Mountains. It is perhaps the most picturesque section of the Pacific Crest Trail in Southern California, at least until it

reaches the southern Sierras. Many hikers snub this NW corner of the Angeles National Forest for no good reason, mistakenly believing it is wasteland with sharp rocky canyons, rounded peaks and no trees. Big mistake—but it's their loss and our gain. I've hiked this trail many times and have run into a few hikers or hunters. Desolate? Sure—but in a good way. I'd describe the area surrounding this trail as achingly beautiful, and it can be hiked comfortably in all seasons. At 5500 feet the summer is refreshing, yet it's low enough to escape heavy snow and extreme cold that you'll experience at over 7500 feet in winter.

It's a 5.2-mile loop trail and worth every step.

Begin your hike from the car on a short descent to the abandoned and primitive Lower Shake Campground. This is where you'll pick up Shake Creek. You'll experience several easy creek crossings as you wend your way up the canyon to Upper Shake Campground. It's a 1.0- mile climb through alders, oaks and pines. Careful: in the canyon along the creek you may encounter abundant clumps of poison oak and stinging nettles. Also, the trail is thin, eroded and slippery along the edge. Shake Creek will continue to babble until you get into the larger pines. Watch for lupine and baby blue eyes. Note: Upper Shake Campground is closed during the winter (and possibly most of the fall and spring), which makes those times great to utilize the trail because the campground will be empty and closed off to traffic, and will serve as an excellent picnic and rest spot coming or going.

Once in the campground, walk along the outer loop road and look for the signed spur trail to the Pacific Crest Trail. On one of my visits it began to snow in slow motion while I sat on a picnic table. Then a blizzard arrived. I was about to turn back when—just like that—it stopped. I was able to make the first tracks in the snow along the Pacific Crest Trail.

I mentioned hunters. This was also the time I encountered a trio. They were after a special migrating duck, which passes high over Sawmill Mountain twice a year. Many hikers dislike hunters, for a myriad of reasons. I believe that hunters need the wilderness just like hikers do, and can be part of an eclectic alliance of different interests that will fight to protect and preserve (as well as purchase) wilderness areas. The more the merrier. Also, the guys I met were considerate and professional. They followed all the rules. They had the best equipment and gear, and handled their rifles expertly and responsibly. I'm not a fan of hunting, but when I see dedicated hunters like these men, I remind myself that they love and respect the outdoors just like me. I also concede that hunting is an American tradition. The more groups that environmental activists can bring into the fight, the more formidable the movement will become. Power in numbers, I say.

Take the signed .25-mile spur trail with switchbacks to the Pacific Crest Trail junction on Sawmill Mountain ridge. You have now gained about 1000 feet altitude from your car. Turn right (NW) on the Pacific Crest and start hiking. This area has steep slopes and is wild and isolated. The trail, however, is reasonably flat. It experiences little traffic. It's also California spotted owl territory. Black oaks, digger/Coulter pines and bigcone Douglas firs line the trail. This two-mile stretch of the West's most famous trail is splendid, with panoramic views of the vast Mojave Desert and snow-capped Tehachapis. Bushwhack about 100 yards toward the ridgeline and you'll be rewarded with views of Castaic Lake and the Santa Clarita Valley. The ridgeline summit runs parallel to the San Andreas Fault, where a whole-lotta-shaking's-going-on.

As you continue to hike on the Pacific Crest Trail, you'll be following a pine and fir whaleback ridge that is serene and delightful, with rugged canyons and steep ravines. Many picnic spots and backpacking campsites are located on the left (NW) side of the trail. My absolutely favorite spot is 0.5 from the spur trail junction. A huge pinnacled rock invites you to climb up and sit. Relax on the rock with a glass of wine or beer in your hand and enjoy the spectacular views and fresh air.

After two miles, a junction on the right will lead back to Upper Shake Campground. Take the access trail back to Lower Shake Canyon and your car.

Hike # 15

Jupiter Peak

> *"Los Angeles was for so long the special end point of the westering dream, the pot of gold at the end of the rainbow... it has received more than its share of restless visionaries and misfits."*
> - Janis P. Stout

Directions – Take I-5 north from the San Fernando Valley for 8 miles and exit at Valencia. Drive east to Bouquet Canyon Road. Turn left (north) and drive to Bouquet Reservoir. Turn left (west) on Spunky Canyon Road. Trail is at Spunky Canyon gap, but is unmarked. Park on left (south) side of road located at mile marker 2.68.

The trailhead for Jupiter Peak—actually there are two peaks—is on the south side of Spunky Canyon Road among a grove of reforested pine, cedar, mountain mahogany and cypress planted in 1964. Unfortunately, the trailhead is unmarked, but it's not too difficult to locate. In the parking area, look southwest or to your right, just past the water tank, and feel your way to the trail, which has a gentle slope along the north side of the taller peak. Do not veer to the left. On my first venture up the peak, I made that mistake and ended up following a steep firebreak to the peak. Wrong trail! I made it to the top, but not without some whining. It was a heart-pounding ascent in the sun. The actual trail to the right is gradual, shady and can be seen from the highway. It's a very pleasant trail through manzanita, chaparral, oak and sage until you reach the saddle between the two peaks.

The twin peaks are Jupiter Peak on the left (SE) at 4498 feet and Jung Peak to the right (NW) at 4431. It's a 1.5-mile hike to the top of Jupiter Peak. That makes 3.0 miles round trip, or 5.6 miles if you also tackle Jung Peak, which I highly recommend.

Some publications call the trail to the peaks, "trail of shin splints," because of the shifting slippery rock. Take it slow and it's not too bad. Always be alert on rocky paths, especially on the way down. I worry much more about ankles or falls than shin splints.

Beautiful wildflowers line the trail in spring.

At the saddle, turn left and scoot up the short but steep rocky slope to Jupiter Peak, a quick 485-foot gain in elevation. On top, enjoy 360-degree views of the Santa Clarita Valley and Bouquet Canyon to the south, Glass Mountain and the town of Green Valley to the northwest, and Bouquet Reservoir, Sierra Pelona, Elizabeth Lake and upper Mojave Desert to the north and northeast. Look for the Pacific Crest Trail on Glass Mountain in the north, and Bouquet pipeline that feeds water from the L.A. aqueduct to Bouquet Reservoir through Cherry Canyon to the south. Pockets of Castaic Lake are also visible to the south.

It may be quite windy on top, with absolutely no shade, so come prepared with hat, sunglasses and sunscreen, even in winter. Take a seat on the small bench provided after signing the hikers register. Walk to the SE rim and observe Bouquet Reservoir sparkling like an emerald at your feet. It appears so close you'll feel like you could toss a good-sized rock into its water. But don't. You could bonk a hiker coming up the firebreak on the noodle. Remember: he's already in a bad mood.

Recently, a group of geo-cachers hid coins on the peak to encourage more hikers. Kennedy half-dollars were used, one of the most popular coins in the world, especially in Germany following JFK's "Ich bin ein Berliner" speech next to the Berlin Wall. A type of pastry, or donut, is really called a Berliner in Germany. I took a picture of a Berliner shop in Cologne, Germany in 2013.

On your way back down to the saddle, please consider climbing Jung Peak. It is more remote and isolated than Jupiter Peak and I believe it's the prettier spot. It only adds 2.6 miles to the hike. Trust me— you'll love it up there. After you bag the second peak, you may return to your car on the same route.

Side note # 1 – You may notice a partial view of Elizabeth Lake to the northeast. The lake was once called Devil's Lake (La Laguna de Diablo) because a

Spanish rancher living nearby believed the devil put a pet monster in the lake. (It was later known as the Elizabeth Lake monster.) Also, it was believed if you swam deep enough in the lake, you could discover a secret passage to hell. "Screams" and other "unnatural noises" coming from the lake at night discouraged others from building lake houses. Throughout history, multiple sightings of the Elizabeth Lake monster have been reported. Described as a giant winged lizard, possibly a relative of a pterodactyl, it was believed to carry off livestock. In the 1880s, two hunters on Jupiter Peak spotted a "winged alligator" flying up a canyon from Elizabeth Lake. Google Elizabeth Lake Monster and read about the many hilarious sightings.

Side note # 2 – In the early 1850s, Elizabeth Lake was a frequent haunt of California grizzly bears—the proud *ursus horribilus* featured on the California state flag. The bears were so numerous that cattle ranching were considered impractical. Unfortunately, the California grizzly bear is now extinct.

Hike # 16

Rice Canyon

> *"This is the city. Los Angeles, California. I work here - I carry a badge. My name's Friday. The story you're about to see is true: the names have been changed to protect the innocent."*
> - Sgt. Joe Friday, *Dragnet*

Directions – Take I-5 north from the San Fernando Valley and drive 5 miles. Exit at Calgrove Boulevard. Turn right (west) on Old Road and drive south 1 mile. Small parking area is on right (west) side of highway. Look for sign.

Rice Canyon Trail is a remarkably resplendent 2.6-mile round-trip hike a mere 10-minute drive north of the San Fernando Valley. This marvelous path is so close to the city you don't have to wait for weekends to enjoy: it would make a perfect trek after work! Rice Canyon is also in the heart of the Santa Clarita Woodlands Preserve and has rich and lush flora. The trail is tucked into a steep box canyon topped with bigcone Douglas fir. You'd never realize that three million people were just down the road—a million miles away in essence.

Be sure to check out the small botanical gardens near the trailhead that features native grasses and other interesting flora. Also, be sure to bring three one-dollar bills for the parking permit. I once arrived in the late afternoon not realizing there was such a fee. I wondered why I saw four or five cars parked out on the highway. I checked my wallet and found three twenties and two ones. What would you have done? Put a twenty into the envelope and hoped a ranger would come by with change? Me neither. Where would he have put the change, on my windshield? Since it was late, I figured officials had already been by and collected for the day, so I put in my two ones with a note explaining my situation. I returned to my car in two hours and discovered a ticket under the wipers. The fine? Seventy-five dollars! Of all the Mickey Mouse citations!! I let out a string of profanities. I vowed to my wife that I wouldn't pay the fine, but when she reminded me that if I didn't I'd have a warrant out for my arrest, I wrote the check.

Start your hike by passing an old water trough, evidence of the former horse and cattle ranch era, and turn up the trail west into Rice Canyon. A sign will show you the way. I don't recommend the hike up East Canyon. It's on an old dirt road and is uphill the entire way. Just when the terrain starts to get pretty, you'll run smack into a locked gate with plenty of Keep Out and No Trespassing signs. The property is still owned by utility companies who don't want the public treading on their land. Hopefully, the parcel will be purchased by the county one day and connect East Canyon to Mission Peak.

Hikers only in Rice Canyon! Good news. That means you won't have to contend with stepping over mushy horse poop or being run over by the lunatic mountain bikers who terrorize East Canyon. Try a late afternoon in spring. It's shadowy and much cooler than summer, plus you may catch a spectacular sunset. The waist-high yellow-green grass glistens in the final glimmer of the sun's rays, while aphids flit about in the cool air. It's a pastoral scene.

Just off the East Canyon trail, you'll encounter a luxuriant and rich meadow. The trail crosses a year-round creek several times as you drift through a forest of willows, sycamores and cottonwoods. Also tucked away in this rolling grassland are evergreens, four varieties of oak, and beautiful wildflowers. Eventually the trail leads to a grassy knoll topped with large oaks and offering lovely views of the box canyon. I'm ashamed to admit that I haven't climbed to the top of the canyon. The routes are steep but doable. If you do make the climb, you'll find yourself in a pine and fir forest, almost unthinkable, being so close to the Valley, and all within the 2000-acre Michael Antonovich Open Space Preserve. The top also straddles several other ridges of the Santa Susanna Mountains—a wild and wooly place. Deer, coyote, bobcat, bear and mountain lion roam the backcountry. Always be aware of the possibility of rattlesnakes, especially in spring and summer, though the threat is minimal. Many publications warn of ticks. Stay on the trails and you'll be fine. If you bushwhack, always check your skin and clothing for the little rascals. Look for quail in the hollows and hawk soaring in the outer limits.

Enjoy a picnic on the grassy knoll.

Side note – Upon leaving the parking lot, turn left (north) and follow signs to the parking area for Wiley and Towsley Canyons. A 5.3-mile loop trail climbs to a picturesque ridge before plunging into Wiley Canyon.

Hike # 17

Mission Peak

"If L.A. has often seemed like a city without history, it is because so much of its history has been recycled into myth."
- David Ulin

Directions – Drive north on Balboa Boulevard in the north San Fernando Valley. One mile past Rinaldi, turn left (west) on Joliette Avenue and cross Sesnon Boulevard, and then make a left on Doric Street. Turn right on Neon Way and follow signs to O'Melveny Park.

Holy cow! Another terrific hike minutes away from the San Fernando Valley. In fact, Mission Peak can be seen from just about any location in the Valley. The hike is a 4.5-mile round trip with a moderately steep climb to the top. Take plenty of breaks. There is little shade and a couple of sections can be heart-pounding. At the top you'll be rewarded with the finest views of the San Fernando Valley.

Mission Peak is 2771 feet high. Though not as popular or well known as Griffith Park, O'Melveny is L.A.s second largest city park. Leashed dogs are allowed on trails. Careful: wildlife includes coyote, bobcat and a very rare mountain lion. Also, there's a healthy rattlesnake population. Stay out of the brush and you will be in little or no danger. Fall, winter and spring usually boast perfect hiking conditions. Summer months can be a roast. Be sure to spend time at the park. It is a passive and serene beauty with no ballfields or playgrounds other than nature. It's a peaceful place to laze and relax. Check out the large number of California walnut trees. After a rainstorm, dust is limited and the wildflowers among the verdant grassland are abundant.

The trail to Mission Peak begins on the north side of the park. Follow signs to Bee Canyon. After .25 miles look for the Peak Trail on the left: it may not be signed. It's still easy to recognize because that's where the ascent begins. Be sure to carry hat, sunglasses, sunscreen and plenty of water.

You will pass through several awesome grasslands.

The hike has a 1325-foot gain in elevation. Many publications rave about the great workout. Wrong attitude, dudes. A workout should not be on a list of hiking priorities.

At the top of the peak are the iconic "three trees," a short row of thick oaks that at last provide shade and an excellent resting spot. Some publications say four oaks: either one has died or somebody doesn't know how to count. The westernmost tree has a box with notes and messages from fellow hikers that you are welcome to read. Feel free to add your own thoughts. Enjoy the fantastic views of the San Fernando Valley and beyond. The sights of the Verdugo and Hollywood Hills and Santa Monica Mountains are splendid. On a clear day, downtown Los Angeles, Mt. Baldy and even glimpses of the Pacific Ocean are possible. Observe the jets coming in at eye-level and banking toward Burbank and Van Nuys airports.

The trail is dedicated to Dr. Mario de Campos, who was a colorful and well-known family physician. A stone memorial on the peak tells his story.

Also, check out Van Norman Dam, practically at your feet to the southeast. The dam was nearly breeched during the 1971 Sylmar earthquake, causing thousands of residents to evacuate their homes, including yours truly. Today, it is the new and improved Los Angeles Reservoir. To the northwest, look for the gas pipes and oil wells on Oat Mountain.

At one time in history Mission Peak overlooked an arid valley dotted with Native American villages, and later horse ranches and vast orange groves. Today the peak stands guard over two million inhabitants amidst the grandeur of suburban sprawl.

Side note – If you dare, slip past the locked gate and No Trespassing signs and hike into a surprisingly sumptuous environment adjacent to the Michael Antonovich Open Space Preserve. You'll find yourself among oak, pine and bigcone Douglas fir, and you may catch a glimpse of a legendary bear who raids nearby subdivisions. Hide if a ranger or gas truck approaches. I can't guarantee you won't be fined or arrested. Open up the area to the public, you creeps—and quit leaking natural gas into the Valley!

Hike # 18

La Tuna Canyon

"L.A. is a metropolis carved from desert and ringed by ocean and mountains, whose pure, flat light can lend a deceptively tranquil quality to an environment where uncontrollable forces remain at work."
- Lawrence Weschler

Directions – Take Exit 14 (La Tuna Canyon) off I-210 and drive 1.4 miles west. Park at the small picnic area on the south side of the highway. Look for the green sign marking the La Tuna Canyon trailhead.

The Verdugo Hills are a mountain island chain in the east San Fernando Valley, and La Tuna Canyon is a lush, challenging and solitary hike that leads to several dandy vistas and even an experimental forest. The views are terrific in nearly every direction. Also, the Verdugo Hills are surrounded by nearly two million residents, most of whom merely glance at the green slopes on the way to work and then don't give them another thought.

La Tuna Canyon Trail is off the beaten path and is not heavily used. The vast majority of Verdugo Hills hikers opt for the Peak Trail, which is an ugly old fire road in view of I-210, but leads directly the top of 3126-foot Verdugo Peak. You'll notice a boatload of cars parked just off the Interstate. Don't worry; all the hikers are heading for the Peak Trail, which is crowded, boring and has little shade. La Tuna Canyon has comparable views and you get to hike through two splendid forested canyons.

Stop at the Grotto Picnic Area for a quick hike to a small waterfall.

La Tuna Canyon Trail is a 4.5-mile round trip to a fire road at the top ridge. It has a 1200- foot elevation gain to the road. It's well worth it to tack on an additional 1.5 miles for a total of 6.0 miles in order to reach the experimental forest, planted after a devastating fire in 1927. If you desire, you can even hike another half-mile to reach Verdugo Peak where you can party with the mobs. La Tuna Canyon is a hilly hike on a narrow trail through Oak and Sycamore Canyons. Good news—dogs are allowed. From the parking area, the trail immediately leads into dense foliage and is lined with sycamore and gnarled oaks forming weird and twisting tunnels. Mountain sage and mint grows in thick clumps. Take a sniff. Sage and mint clear your mind and soul of negative thoughts and energy. Also, poison oak thrives. My advice—stay on the trail.

At 0.8 miles you'll reach a plateau with views to the east of I-210 and the San Gabriel Mountains. After a short descent, the trail crosses a creek and enters an even lusher canyon with larger sycamore. Here you will start climbing in earnest up a series of switchbacks. Remember: never shortcut on a switchback—it causes erosion and will ruin the trail. La Tuna Canyon Trail is beautifully designed, but does show signs of erosion from flooding and pinheaded hikers who shortcut. This section of the trail is the steepest and can be vigorous. Take your time and rest frequently. You'll pass several old rusted cars from bygone days that were either driven or pushed off the roads and would be a major headache to haul off. As you climb, unfolding views of the San Fernando Valley, Hollywood Hills and Santa Monica Mountains will emerge. Many more incredible views can be found on the Verdugo Fire Road, along with large boulders to scramble up and stretch out on. The elevation on the fire road is 2646 feet. This dirt and gravel access lane is also called Backbone Road.

Continue hiking south, if you choose to go further, and head toward the wondrous experimental forest—a beautiful grove of pine, cedar and cypress nearly 100 years old. Easy and excellent bushwhacking opportunities abound, with loads of blackberry vines and comfortable shady resting areas.

Unfortunately, suburbia is encroaching on the Verdugo Hills, but thankfully the steep canyons and ravines should keep the area safe from development. In most areas it would be too expensive and darn near impossible, even by L.A.s idiotic standards, to build housing tracts.

Side note – I saw my one and only mountain lion at the experimental forest. It was early morning and I was waiting for the sun to clear the San Gabriels. I know the big cat saw me first because when I finally spotted him he was already standing as still as a stone among the pines and staring at me. His long tail swished back and forth and his eyes seemed to glow. Much to my relief, he appeared bored by my presence and finally trotted off to the south. I was surprised by the big cat's presence because he had to cross several busy streets to gain access to the Verdugo Hills. Perhaps, however, nothing should ever be surprising in the eerie solar system known as Los Angeles.

Hike # 19

Chumash Trail

"In Los Angeles you get the sense sometimes there's a mysterious patrol at night: when the streets are empty and everyone's asleep, they go cruising past. It's like a Ray Bradbury story."
- Carlos Ruiz Zafon

Directions – From the north San Fernando Valley, drive west on the 118 and exit at Yosemite Avenue. Drive 0.4 miles to Flanagan Drive. Turn right and continue 0.8 miles to trailhead on right (east) side of street. Park on east side of the road and not in front of residences.

In 1990 the Santa Monica Mountains Conservancy negotiated a deal to purchase a 4369- acre parcel overlooking the Simi and San Fernando Valleys in the northwest section of Chatsworth. The owner who sold the property was iconic entertainer and comedian Bob Hope.

Our hike is a rolling 5.3-mile round trip that can be extended in any direction at the top of the ridge. The trail has very light traffic, since for some inexplicable reason most hikers use the trailhead directly off the 118 and hike north. It's baffling to me. Most of that trail is on an unimpressive fire road and is not nearly as pleasant or picturesque as the Chumash Trail. But the final destination is the same—Rocky Point, a 2715-foot legendary peak with an 1100-foot elevation gain from Flanagan Drive. It's a slightly steeper climb off the 118.

Horses and mountain bikers are allowed to roam, so be wary. Always give way to horses. That seems pretty obvious since a horse is quite large and I'd rather not be kicked, bitten or stomped on by an animal as big as a pickup. Mountain bikers must lawfully give way to hikers, but rarely do, and it takes guts to stand your ground. The best news is that leashed dogs are allowed on the trail.

Early mornings in the Santa Susannahs are often cool and foggy, and that's a great time to get the uphill out of the way, especially in summer. The trail boasts very little if any shade, so plan accordingly. Lean against rocks at the top to block the sun. Summer can be harsh. I believe summers in L.A. were created so people would go to the beach or high mountains.

Through much of the winter and spring, wildflowers are riotous and the hills a velvet green, similar to the rolling hills near the coast of Ireland. At times the area can be stunning. It's a moderately difficult hike to the ridge, mostly uphill but not overly demanding. Deer, coyote and fox prance among the tall sandstone features. Large hawks soar in the sky. As usual, publications warn of rattlesnakes. Of course they're out here, but you probably won't see one.

At the summit of Rocky Peak, the Pacific Ocean and Channel Islands are visible on a clear day. You'll also have excellent views of Simi Valley and much of the Santa Susannahs. To climb and bushwhack along Rocky Peak ridge is both challenging and enjoyable fun. Be persistent in locating the actual peak, as there are many false peaks. The highest pile of boulders is what you seek. Rocky Peak is the boundary between Los Angeles and Ventura counties.

Enjoy the vastness and solitude.

Side note - On my most recent excursion to Rocky Peak, two emergency helicopters hovered over my head. I figured they were searching for someone in need. When I flashed them thumbs up, they moved on. About a half-mile away they hovered again and this time evacuated two people. The entire spectacle was impressive and sobering. When you are hiking these trails you need to be cautious, alert and wary. Backcountry ethics say, "Never do something stupid unless it's absolutely necessary." In the wild it is your responsibility *not* to get hurt. Never perform little stunts that begin with, "Here, hold my beer." If you are injured and require aid or an evacuation, you could endanger your friends or rescuers. Please take care.

Hike # 20

Simi Peak

"The final story, the final chapter of western man, I believe, lies in Los Angeles."
                       - Phil Ochs

Directions – Drive west on U.S. 101 past Los Virgenes Canyon Road and exit at Kanan Road. Drive north 2.2 miles to Sunnycrest Drive. Turn right on Double Tree. Trail entrance is 0.8 miles on the right side of street. Curbside parking only. Look for sign to recreation trail.

At 2405 feet, Simi Peak is the highest summit in the Simi Hills and overlooks the towns of Simi Valley to the north and Thousand Oaks/Moorpark to the west.

      Our hike to the peak traverses perhaps the finest wilderness area totally surrounded by a choking suburbia in the entire United States. Despite the close proximity of strip malls, interstates and cookie-cutter housing tracts, the hike is an absolute triumph, and provides hikers with a remote getaway at civilization's front door. Most hikers have little realization of the actual desolation and incredible beauty of the area. China Flats is a jewel. Other highlights include a fine wilderness canyon (Palo Comado), a pond and, of course, Simi Peak.

Please do not take the trail from Oak Canyon Park as a shortcut to China Flats. You'll be disappointed. It's a 900-foot elevation gain consisting of boring switchbacks on a gravel fire road with views of people's backyards and Hwy101—and it does the 900 feet in one mile. Our trail is a customized hike that will lead through nearly 4500 acres of former Simi Hills ranchland choked with valley oak habitat and radiant native savannahs all protected and supervised by the National Park Service within the Santa Monica Mountains National Recreation Area, and it's slowly expanding thanks to persistent land purchases. It's also dog friendly. A seasonal creek borders China Flats, a wide and enchanting grassland filled with wonderful shady oaks. Opportunities abound to hike the neighboring hills and canyons at a later date—be sure to take note.

This may not be a comfortable hike in the summer. The sun can be torrid. Try spring when the wildflowers are abloom and grass is a light emerald, or winter, which is cooler and will have far fewer fellow hikers.

To begin the 7.8-mile round-trip hike, follow the trail from the street 0.5 miles over a grassy knoll and hook up with Palo Comado Canyon. Turn left (north) on a small dirt road and hike through an impressive stand of sycamore and live oak. Take stock of your surroundings. You're barely a half mile from suburbia, yet you won't see power lines or poles, water tanks or cell phone towers—only trees, hills, deer, fox, bobcat and hawk.

At 1.5 miles start your ascent out of Palo Comado Canyon and take in the view of what you've just hiked through. Look for the historic sheep corral on the right side (north) of the trail. At 3.3 miles you'll finish a short descent and enter China Flats. Note the reflecting pond on the left, which is actually an old stock watering hole.

China Flats is an underrated and often ignored paradise. You can melt away hours by relaxing or playing in this cool, shaded and lovely oak grove. Wander off the trail and explore; it's impossible to get lost. Be a kid again. Then hike up the final 0.5 miles to the top of Simi Peak. The trail is narrow and steep, but not too difficult. Unfortunately, the rocky nature of the trail can be an ankle-twister, so be careful and stay alert, especially on the final 200 yards. At the top are fantastic views of the Santa Monicas, Santa Susannahs and Simi and Conejo Valleys. Look northeast for Bard Lake or east toward the San Fernando Valley and its likely billows of smog. Not on top of Simi Peak, however, where the air is fresh and clean. I've hiked up to the peak three times and may have seen five other people.

Return to your car following the same trail.

Hike # 21

Sandstone Peak – Mishe Mokwa Trail

"How small we feel, with our petty ambitions and strivings, in the presence of the great elemental forces of nature."
— Sherlock Holmes

*"L.A. woman, L.A. woman,
Are you a lucky little lady
From the City of Lights?
Or just another lost angel?
City of Night, City of Night."*
— The Doors

Directions – Drive northwest on CA-1 (Pacific Coast Highway). One mile past the Los Angeles county line, turn right on Yerba Buena Road. Drive 6 miles north to trailhead on left (north) side of road. There's plenty of parking on right side (south) of road.

The Mishe Mokwa Trail is the centerpiece trail in the Santa Monica Mountains and is a MUST trail for all L.A. hikers. It has everything—peaks, pinnacles, boulders, meadows and views—plus, unfortunately, crowds. Try a weekday morning for luck.

Mishe Mokwa translates as Mother Bear. At 3111 feet, Sandstone Peak is the "It" mountain and highest point in the Santa Monica Mountains. It is the focal point of the old Circle X Ranch property, 1655 acres of National Park Service land straddling the L.A.-Ventura county line. Mishe Mokwa is also a premier Southern California trail with easy ascents, several side trails and a feeling of desolation without being lonely or spooky. Because of its popularity, I cannot guarantee a solitary trek, but it is a necessary hike for the L.A. enthusiast, with many notable and memorable features including stunning views of the Pacific Ocean, Point Dume, Channel Islands, Boney Mountains and the picturesque community of Malibu.

The Mishe Mokwa is a 6.1-mile loop trail. You could get to Sandstone Peak in a much speedier 1.5 miles—but what for? You'd be missing the finest trail in the Santa Monica's.

Begin your hike with a .25-mile climb on a fire road, and then turn right onto the Mishe Mokwa Trail. It's a beautifully designed and engineered trail that climbs and descends the brushy slopes of the Boney Mountains. At the beginning, much of the chaparral and manzanita are shoulder high, and the coastal sage proliferates along the trail. Peek over the chaparral for a glimpse of Carlisle Canyon.

This was Chumash Native American territory in the 1600-1700s. Chumash means "seashell people."

Modern names with Chumash origin include Malibu, Ojai, Pismo, Mugu, Simi and Castaic. The Chumash were excellent ocean fisherman and even developed planked canoes called tomols to ply the sea. On land, they dressed up like deer and grazed among a herd until close enough to use their arrows. Spanish soldiers and old world diseases decimated the Chumash population. A revolt in 1824 was crushed and the remaining Chumash were indentured on Mexican haciendas. Today the Chumash population is less than 5,000. The last native speaker of their language died in 1965. The Mishe Mokwa Trail and several other paths in the area were used by tribal members for hundreds of years. Our path descends into Carlisle Canyon with striking views of red volcanic formations, including Balancing Rock and Echo Cliffs. Sycamore, laurel and oak line the trail. Balancing Rock is a remarkable sight with the urgent feeling that a slight breeze might topple it. Look for climbers on the Echo Cliffs.

Next you'll reach Split Rock Trail Camp, an ideal and shady picnic/rest spot with a year-round creek, tables and historic "four-holer" outhouse. As for me? I prefer the wind and bushes to those stinky things.

Split Rock has a small gap large enough to walk-through. It is a custom of the Boy Scouts of America to squeeze through the opening of Split Rock as an act of solidarity. You are welcome to participate in their tradition.

The trail ascends out of the canyon for enjoyable and spectacular views of Point Mugu State

Park, Boney Ridge and Egyptian Rock. It's uphill, but not overly strenuous, with a 1600- foot elevation gain over the entire 6.1 miles. Take the short spur trail to Inspiration Point for striking views of San Clemente and Anacapa Islands. Be sure not to take the cut-off to Boney Ridge. Return to the main trail and head for Sandstone Peak.

As you make a sweeping turn toward the ocean, watch for another spur trail on the right that will lead up to Sandstone Peak. It is not signed. If you have difficulty locating the spur, simply wait a few minutes and another group of hikers will probably be along to help. Once again, if solace is what you seek, this may not be your favorite trail—but you must experience the summit of Sandstone Peak, a craggy volcanic mass that is dazzling.

Spring will have an explosion of wildflowers.

At the summit, check out the plaque that honors W. Herbert Allen, a Circle X Ranch owner. (The Boy Scouts named the peak Mt. Allen, but it never caught on.) Also, look for California condors soaring over the Topatopa Mountains to the northeast. Sign the registry to be a part of history. The Sierra Club regularly replaces and sends the records to the Bancroft Library in Berkeley. Heather Brady signed the registry and reminded hikers that it can be brutally hot in summer. "Hotter than the crevices of Satan's butt cheeks," she wrote. Quite descriptive, Heather!

Take the final 1.5 miles downhill to the parking area.

Hike # 22

Lower Solstice Canyon and Sostomo Trail

"Malibu! With sounds of waves crashing, and the ocean at the doorstep, you feel like you are hours away from civilization - and with L.A traffic, you ARE!"
- Jennifer Harrison

Directions – From Malibu drive 2.2 miles northwest on CA-1 (Pacific Coast Highway). Turn right on Corral Canyon Road. Drive 0.2 miles and turn left at entrance sign. It is 0.3 miles to parking area. Free parking! But with only fifty spaces, the lot is often filled, which says something about the potential crowds. Overflow parking is available.

Hiking through lower Solstice Canyon, and then up the Sostomo Trail to Deer Valley Loop, is a 5.8-mile round-trip hike. You'll pass a cool waterfall (most of the crowds hang around this spot), ruins of a historical residence and finally wind your way up to a remote and breathtaking 1.3-mile loop trail that takes you high above the Pacific Ocean. The first 1.2 miles are easy and scenic, and a total joy unless the area is packed with screeching children and Griswold type adults. The trail is wide, wheelchair accessible and dog friendly.

Your first destination is the remains of what is called Tropical Terrace, a formerly beautiful Malibu hideaway that once boasted a private zoo with exotic animals such as camels and giraffes. Unfortunately, like so many other hillside homes, the huge residence fell victim to a devastating 1982 fire. Formerly known as Robert's Ranch (Fred and Florence), the National Park Service Administration took over under the auspices of the Santa Monica Mountains National Recreation Area.

Before you reach Tropical Terrace, look for the 1865 stone cottage on the right side of trail. It's the oldest existing stone building in the Malibu community. At one time it was known as the Matthew Keller house. Stroll through the lush bay, alder, oak and sycamore groves along the trail. Many of the trees are quite old and large. Also note the fabulous palms at Tropical Terrace.

Once you reach Tropical Terrace, or old Robert's Ranch, the agave, bamboo and bird of paradise will amaze you. The home was built in 1952 by African-American architect Paul Revere Williams, who designed more than 2000 homes in Los Angeles, including ones for Lucille Ball, Barbara Stanwyck and Frank Sinatra. He even designed the Shrine Auditorium and iconic theme buildings at Los Angeles International Airport.

A statue of the Virgin Mary at Tropical Terrace is a pleasant spot to rest up for the long climb. Be sure to scramble over the rocks and check out the creek and waterfall. Just follow the screaming children. Watch for poison oak and bright green wild parrots.

I freely admit the area could be creepy after dark, with many ghostly haunts among the old structures. Spooky stories have been circulated of vaporous figures wandering the trails. Perhaps one day the park service will organize evening candlelight ghost tours. Chumash, Spanish and Mexican ghosts purportedly inhabit the canyon.

The waterfall has a tropical grotto on Solstice Creek and there are even ruins of an old bomb shelter, remnant of the 1950s duck-and-cover days with Bert the Turtle. The children can be noisy. I know, they're just kids, and what a great time they have running and climbing among the creek, falls and ruins, but they're still annoying. It's time to move on and head up the Sostomo Trail. The lonely 1.3-mile Deer Valley Loop Trail will be the highlight of your day.

Climb the west wall of Solstice Canyon, descend to Shady Creek, and then start up the east wall. Note: at least two burned-out cabins await your exploration just off short spur trails. Please be careful among the ruins.

Finally, you'll climb up a steep and rugged slope to the Deer Valley Loop. This is a special hike—do not miss it! Hike in either direction, though I prefer going to the right so that fine coastal views of the Malibu community, Palos Verde Point and Santa Catalina Island are near the end of the loop. And it's all downhill without the sun in your face. It's a delightful and picturesque trail that can be done over and over again. Be sure to enjoy an adult beverage on this section of the hike. Wine or beer and Pacific Ocean! And no kids!

Return the same way you came.

Side note – Many splendid restaurants abound in the Malibu region of the PCH, all inviting hungry hikers to lunch or dinner. Moonshadows and Sunset Restaurant are elegant and pricey, but well worth a visit. The Paradise Cove Beach Cafe has great food and you'll recognize the views of the point from movies and countless commercials. My recommendation is Neptune's Nest just off of Yerba Linda Road, established in 1956, for a fine taste of old Malibu, or the Malibu Pier Restaurant with its spectacular views of surfers carving up the waves at America's most famous surfing beach.

Hike # 23

Nicholas Flat

*"Perhaps there is no life after death...
there is just Los Angeles."*
- Kevyn L.

Directions – Drive 12 miles northwest from Malibu on CA-1 (Pacific Coast Highway) and turn right (north) on Highway 23 (Decker Road). Go 2.5 miles to Decker School Road and turn left (west). Drive to the end of Decker School Road and park.

Nicholas Flat is a small oak woodland paradise complete with meadows, oak hammocks and an old cattle-watering pond, all tucked away in a secluded and charming corner of the Santa Monica Mountains. Several sandstone lookouts have "wow" views of the Pacific Ocean, Zuma Beach, Point Dume and neighboring hills. The meadows are gorgeous grasslands like the ones seen in the movies *Dances with Wolves* and *Legends of the Fall*—yet all in the Santa Monica Mountains National Recreation Area. Coastal sage and mint are an overwhelming olfactory presence.

    The tiny flat is hit or miss with crowds. Weekends often bring the hordes, so try a weekday. Either way, it's a pleasant outing with plenty of hidden spots to be alone. Spring can be fresh from winter rains, and the meadows will be green and lush with an explosion of wildflowers.

From your car, hike south to the pond and search for the bedrock mortar holes where the Chumash milled acorns. No signs offer help, so just feel your way along the trail and you'll find it. It's impossible to get lost because the acreage isn't large enough. Explore the shoreline of the pond and its many shaded spots to stretch out and relax. Beware of the large clumps of poison oak. Some bloggers complain about the pond being dry. I've visited Nicholas Flat five times and the pond has always had sparkling water. Along the shoreline, a short spur trail leads to a small peak with eye-popping views of the cliffs and ocean. An ocean breeze with salt and Pacific spray will hit you in the face. Several other knobs along the trail, between 1600-1800 feet, have similar views of the coast and beaches.

Many publications recommend the 7.0-mile round trip trail from Leo Carrillo State Park. Not me. That trail is steep, with an elevation gain of 1600 feet and virtually no shade. Many on-line posts rave about the trail's "killer workout." Dudes, gimme a break! Hiking should not be part of a training schedule, that's what 10K road races are for. Hiking is a wonderment and enjoyment. It's a spiritual and mystical experience—physical fitness benefits are just the cherry on top. You want a workout, go to the gym. Trail experiences can be ruined by rude and speedy hikers or thoughtless mountain bikers who ignore their surroundings and only seek a killer workout.

Leo Carrillo State Park is a fine place to visit after your hike at Nicholas Flat. Carrillo was a TV western star, famous for playing the Cisco Kid's sidekick Pancho, who rode a beautiful palomino named Loco. He was also the son of Santa Monica's first mayor.

The state park has an excellent picnic area where you can watch the surfers ride the point break waves on the other side of the PCH. The entire area is picturesque.

However, Nicholas Flat is the star of this outing, and the trail off Decker School Road is easier and much more accommodating. The coastal community of wildflowers includes purple sage, bush lupine, holly leaf, red berry and gooseberry. Deer, fox, coyote and bobcat slip through the grassy meadows. My favorite thing to do is to loll about in a shady spot and enjoy the oak-ringed flat. It is drop-dead gorgeous and you'll feel far away from the world and its woes. It's a place for all sorts of adult activities. Parts of the trail may be overgrown. I always recommend wearing long pants on trails where you might be brushing up against vegetation that could sting, scratch or poison, and may be loaded with ticks.

After your hike, head back down to the PCH and turn south for a delicious dinner at Malibu Seafood Restaurant. The place is one of those many restaurants that appear to be a grubby hole-in-the-wall, but the food is as good as the most expensive restaurants on the coast!

Hike # 24

Sycamore and Serrano Canyons

"Two girls grew up at the edge of the ocean near L.A. and knew it was paradise, and better than Eden, which was only a garden."
- Eve Babitz

Directions – Drive north from Malibu 32 miles on CA-1 (Pacific Coast Highway) to Big Sycamore Canyon Campground at Point Mugu State Park. Many publications recommend parking on the PCH in order to escape paying a park entrance fee. Give me a break, cheapskates! The money supports our state parks. Plus, your vehicle will be much safer from thieves and vandals inside the park. Walk past the campground to the gate in order to start your hike.

At over 14,000 acres and with sixty miles of trails, Point Mugu State Park is the largest and most continuous preserved area in the Santa Monica Mountains National Recreation Area.

Begin your 8.5-mile loop by hiking up Sycamore Canyon. It has a fine year-round creek running down its center and—go figure—magnificent sycamores. Many are huge specimens over 100 feet tall;

they make up the largest clustering in the state of California. Watch for hawks and owls relaxing on the branches.

In fall this is butterfly country, with giant monarchs on their winter migration to Southern and Baja California colonies. Best viewing is further up Sycamore Canyon. Not only do butterflies taste bad, but they make birds sick so they learn not to eat them. Cool! Too bad humans lack that ability. Can you imagine a Great White Shark or Bengal Tiger looking at us and saying, "Yuck"? In the animal kingdom, bright colors are a warning, not an invitation. Also in fall, believe it or not, Southern California has a changing of the leaves, and it is nowhere more evident than in Sycamore Canyon, where the leaves turn orange, yellow and ecru before falling.

After hiking 1.5 miles up Sycamore Canyon, with its very wide path, turn right onto the slim Serrano Canyon trail. Publications delight in warning of ticks and poison oak, and then proceed to encourage bushwhacking and scrambling off the trail to find pools along the creek. Hello! What you'll find by the creek are—duh—ticks and poison oak. The only time ticks and poison oak become a hazard is when a hiker, perhaps after too many lattes, decides to romp off the trail and into the bush like an Irish setter. Stay on the trail! Don't wade through bushes you can't identify. If you're like me, that's a majority of them.

Be on the lookout for deer, coyote and bobcat.

Serrano Canyon is rarely crowded. It's an ignored treasure. The trail passes through a canyon with many huge oaks and leads to a stunning grassland that is arguably the most picturesque in the entire Santa Monicas. Publications complain and warn of spider webs draped across the narrow trail. Dudes—that means no other hikers have come by recently. Rejoice! Serrano Canyon also has the finest native tall grass in the state.

The canyon is extremely narrow and densely wooded with oak, laurel and smaller sycamore. The canyon is also a dramatic walled gorge with an easy to moderate climb for about one mile up to the grassland. At the top of the canyon, cross an old fence line and enter the beautiful grass prairie. This is my favorite part of the hike. It's vast and desolate, and makes you feel like you've entered a time warp into the 19th century. Serrano Canyon can be spooky if you're alone, but there have been no ghost or mountain lion sightings in years. Once in the grasslands, delight to the sound of birds and winds swishing through the golden, yellow, red and green grasses. Look for an old water shed and pump. In these grasslands you'll be totally exposed to the sun so bring hat, sunscreen and sunglasses. I do not recommend summer hiking in the area.

As you slowly ascend to the gap, you'll pass an abandoned cabin. Do not take the Serrano Valley Trail on the right. Continue up to the top of the ridge where you'll discover awesome views of the Boney Mountains and Boney Mountain Ridge, perhaps the most striking and spectacular outcrops in the Santa Monicas. At the top of the ridge, with an overall elevation gain of 850 feet, you'll finally reach the gap and see the back section of Sycamore Canyon far below. Wind your way to the bottom. The trail is not as steep as it looks, or as difficult as some publications suggest. Heck, it's only downhill!

Side note – Serrano Canyon was named for Jesus Serrano, a small farmer in the area who, much like St. Christopher, was noted for his hospitality to weary travelers. Serrano was dirt poor, yet kind and generous with whatever he had. How many of the wealthy hacendados would do the same thing? Why is it always the poor who help other people? They are the salt of the earth. They are warm, friendly and hospitable while so many of the wealthy are snooty, arrogant and live behind locked gates. There's something to be said about a camel never passing through the eye of a needle that makes perfect sense.

When you reach the bottom of Sycamore Canyon and creek, it's a flat and pleasant 4.0- mile stretch back to your car. There are several picnic spots with tables along the way. Enjoy!

Hike # 25

Mt. Baldy

"The whole city gives you the impression of impermanence. You have the feeling that one day someone is going to yell, "Cut! Strike it!" And then the stagehands will scurry out and remove the mountains, movie star homes, the Hollywood Bowl - everything."
- Allan Sherman

Directions – From Upland, exit off I-10 or I-210 and drive north on Old Baldy Road to Manker Flats Campground. Follow signs to trailhead.

Three saintly mountains tower to the east of the City of Angels—San Gorgonio (11,503 feet), San Jacinto (10,834 feet) and San Antonio. The smallest, at 10,068 feet, but by far the best known and most difficult hike, is Mt. San Antonio, more popularly known as Mt. Baldy. Baldy is still the tallest peak in the San Gabriels and is visible from much of the Los Angeles area and San Fernando Valley on clear days. In summer, its bald head dazzles from white stones which resembles snow. In winter, it is snow.

Padres at Mission San Gabriel named the mountain San Antonio in 1790 after St. Anthony of

Padua. In the 1870s, gold was discovered in the area and prospectors dubbed the peak Old Baldy.

Mt. Baldy is king of the Southern California peaks. It is the most striking mountain south of the Sierras. Every Southern California hiker *must*, at one time, make the pilgrimage up Baldy's steep and sublime slopes.

Careful: it could be 100 degrees in Upland, and hot and sweaty on the ascent—yet have freezing temperatures and severe winds at the top. Come prepared.

The hike is 8.4 miles round trip with an elevation gain of 3900 feet. Some sections of the trail are quite steep, and the air is thin. Take it slow and steady—the hike is not a race. From Manker Flats, hike 0.9 miles along the ski lift road to the Ski Hut Trail on the left. Be alert and watch for the small sign—it's easy to miss. The Ski Hut Trail climbs a series of switchbacks that appear to be endless. Once again, no need to rush. Enjoy the views and conserve your energy. You are climbing through upper San Antonio Canyon. You'll pass sugar, Jeffrey and lodgepole pines, and white and bigcone Douglas fir.

At 2.5 miles you'll reach the Sierra Club's San Antonio Ski Hut, built in 1937 by Sierra Club mountaineers. You can actually spend the night. (For reservations call 213-387-4287.) It's a great spot to relax and rest up for the next part of the climb. Beyond the ski hut is an open rocky bowl that crosses a creek and rock garden. Careful: do not scamper over the rocks—falls can be treacherous. On the opposite side of the rock garden you'll begin another stiff round of fewer but longer switchbacks.

Bighorn sheep can reputedly be spotted starting at 8500 feet. I saw none. Watch for deer and black bear. Black bear did not naturally exist in the San Gabriel's, but in 1933 eleven "bad boy" bears from Yosemite National Park were released near Crystal Lake and have proliferated. Think of the San Gabriels as the original bear detention center. Grizzly bear once roamed Mt. Baldy. In fact, a grizzly bear is featured on the California state flag. They were once common, but today no grizzly exists in California. The last grizzly bear was shot by Walter L. Richardson in 1922. Good job, Walt—you jackass!

At 3.2 miles you'll reach the top of South Ridge. It's now a steep, rocky and twisting 1.0- mile trail to the peak. If you feel that you've left or lost the trail, simply point yourself toward the peak and head up. You'll make it.

The summit is bald. Who would've guessed? Delight in the exquisite views in every direction. On clear days you can spot a very tiny L.A. skyline. Several trails lead back down, but don't even think about taking one. On one path you could slide 1200 feet on scree and end up in the hospital, or worse, while another is a nice enough hike along the Devil's Backbone trail to the ski lift, which will probably not be running. You'll then have to tread down the boring service road.

Some publications claim Mt. Baldy is a sinister and haunted mountain. Really? Google Mt. Shasta. Baldy does have a somewhat "creepy" legend about a population of "little people" dwelling on its slopes. In a spooky episode of a TV reality show called *Legends and Haunts*, producers supposedly found Jacob Shinner's grave (1827-1877) off a small path on Mt. Baldy. Shinner was purportedly a diminutive gold prospector with a mine at nearby Hogback Slide. On a scant path called Party Rock Trail (sounds like a teen urban legend) was an abandoned house with dozens of tiny 5 x 5 rooms and four-foot ceilings. Some called it Shinner's House, or the Gingerbread House. It is also reported that a local witch had lived there. Legend also claims that dwarfs occupied a hidden village on Mt. Baldy, and if you found its location they'd murder you. Yipes! Others claim the dwarf town was actually located on a rocky outcrop east of Riverside, just south of Mt. Baldy. Still others claim the little town housed aliens.

Good luck with all that.

Return to your car using the same route. Four miles south is the Buckhorn Lodge. It has a fabulous home-style restaurant with ice-cold beer, outdoor patio and weekend entertainment. Wow! Great place to wind down after your hike. Cheers!

Epilogue

We Have To Care

"What a country chooses to save is what a country chooses to say about itself."
- Mollie Beattie

As citizens of the United States of America, we must do everything in our power, and more, to protect and defend the American landscape. We have to do it, you and I, there is nobody else.

We have to care.

"I am a patriot of the North American continent."
- Utah Phillips

Happy Trails

"All that the sun shines on is beautiful, so long as it is wild."
- John Muir

Happy trails to you, until we meet again.

Happy trails to you, keep smilin' until then.

Who cares about the clouds when we're together?

Just sing a song and bring the sunny weather.

Happy trails to you, till we meet again.

(From "Happy Trails" by Dale Evans Rogers)

Los Angeles

A meteor from Heaven upon
The heights of the Sierras shone,
As if it were a beam astray,
Shot forth from the eternal day!
And on mountains, weird and old,
Night, awed, her starry rosary told,
And swelled a song that seemed to say,
In ecstasy of blessedness,
Los Angeles, Los Angeles.

- James Abraham Martling

Recommended Reading

1. *The Big Sleep*, Raymond Chandler

2. *Afoot and Afield in Los Angeles County*, Jerry Schad

3. *Day Hiker's Guide to Southern California*, John McKinney

4. *100 Classic Hikes in Southern California*, Allen Reidel

5. *Tales of Ordinary Madness*, Charles Bukowski

6. *Day Hikes Around Los Angeles*, Robert Stone

7. *Writing Los Angeles: A Literary Anthology*, David Ulin, Editor

8. *Favorite Dog Hikes In and Around Los Angeles*, Wynne Benti and Julie Rush

9. *Ecstatic Trails: The 52 Best Day Hikes and Native Walks In and Around Los Angeles*, Rob Campbell

10. *Double Indemnity*, James M. Cain

Acknowledgements

I wish to express my sincere and profound appreciation for the stunningly beautiful area surrounding Los Angeles.

Thank you to my Los Angeles hiking buddies: Greystone Holt, Bobby Kent, Chris Kent, Larry Larson, Kevyn Loveless, Art Schiro, James Lindsay, Liz Kimura, Mike Newman, Richard Knapp, Gary Greenfield, Cyndra Joi Anderson, Coqui Kent, John McKelligot, Danny Dunham, Georganne Alex and Elaine Springer Kent.

Special thanks to Dan Barth, my editor and brother-in-arms.

Back cover photo of G. Kent on Mt. Pinos by Chris Kent.

About The Author

G. Kent lives in the wilds near the Ocala National Forest in North Florida. He was born and raised in Los Angeles. He is also the author of *Running with Razors and Soul: A Handbook for Competitive Runners* (Bandit Press, 2013), *Hiking in North Florida with William Bartram, Volumes One* and *Two* (Bandit Press, 2014-2015) and a novel *Grinners* (Bandit Press, 2014).

For more information contact kentib@earthlink.net.

Made in the USA
Las Vegas, NV
02 December 2020